Avidly Reads THEORY

Avidly Reads

General Editors: Sarah Mesle and Sarah Blackwood

The Avidly Reads series presents brief books about how culture makes us feel. We invite readers and writers to indulge feelings—and to tell their stories—in the idiom that distinguishes the best conversations about culture.

Avidly Reads Theory
Jordan Alexander Stein

Avidly Reads Making Out
Kathryn Bond Stockton

Avidly Reads Board Games
Eric Thurm

Theory

JORDAN ALEXANDER STEIN

NEW YORK UNIVERSITY PRESS *New York*

NEW YORK UNIVERSITY PRESS
New York
www.nyupress.org

References to Internet websites (URLs) were accurate at the time
of writing. Neither the author nor New York University Press is
responsible for URLs that may have expired or changed since the
manuscript was prepared.

Library of Congress Cataloging-in-Publication Data
Names: Stein, Jordan Alexander, author.
Title: Avidly reads theory / Jordan Alexander Stein.
Description: New York : New York University Press, [2019] |
Series: Avidly reads | Includes bibliographical references and
index.
Identifiers: LCCN 2019006920| ISBN 9781479827398 (hbk : alk.
paper) | ISBN 9781479801008 (pbk : alk. paper)
Subjects: LCSH: Theory (Philosophy) | Culture.
Classification: LCC B842 .S73 2019 | DDC 140—dc23
LC record available at https://lccn.loc.gov/2019006920

New York University Press books are printed on acid-free paper,
and their binding materials are chosen for strength and durabil-
ity. We strive to use environmentally responsible suppliers and
materials to the greatest extent possible in publishing our books.

Manufactured in the United States of America

10 9 8 7 6 5 4 3 2 1

Also available as an ebook

For Sarah and Sarah

Theory is always a detour on the way
to something more important.

—Stuart Hall

Contents

Preface   xiii

1. Silly Theory   1

2. Stupid Theory   23

3. Sexy Theory   47

4. Seething Theory   75

5. Stuck Theory   99

Coda   125

Acknowledgments   129

Works Consulted   133

About the Author   141

Preface

Few things capture the tenor of my bookish youth better than Feminist Ryan Gosling. This celebrated meme (first on Tumblr, later collected into a book), created by University of Wisconsin graduate student Danielle Henderson, features dashing photos of the Canadian actor captioned by insights from academic feminist theory. When Feminist Ryan Gosling, frocked in a light-blue, collared shirt, looked softly back through my computer screen one spring day in 2011 to say, "Hey Girl. Just thinking about Chandra Mohanty's theory that Western feminism problematically constructs the Third World woman as the pejorative 'other' and the discursive colonial habits that keep women oppressed," I saw nothing so much as myself in 1998. And, Reader, it is not because I look like Ryan Gosling.

The theory that animates this meme also animated my college days. Back then "theory" was the name for an identity: an idea of how to be, a way to live your life. We used the term also to refer to the idiom that expressed the identity—"theory" named a way of thinking and talking about language, power, and history, drawing on a canon of mostly European-educated scholars, philosophers, and psychoanalysts (or, as we called them all, theorists): the likes of Jacques Derrida, Michel Foucault, Roland Barthes, Julia Kristeva, and Jacques Lacan.

Both this idiom and this life plan gathered meaning from their use. Never mind what defined "theory" in any certain terms or what criteria distinguished a theorist from a mere philosopher or critic. What mattered to us was that mastering theory—being, as the common sobriquet identified us, "theory heads"—was a way of recognizing fellow pilgrims en route to the same promised land. Theory's singular idiolect gave my friends and me, in our youth, a springboard for thinking about whatever was to come after youth. Theory offered us a way of understanding the world that, like so many youthful exuberances, was equal parts vital and ridiculous. Verbose abstractions were things out of which we built concrete friendships. They fueled the experiments that we conducted with living and loving, eating and dreaming, doing and having.

I was studious enough in college eventually to become a professor myself, but "studious" didn't exactly mean "serious." Rather, like Feminist Ryan Gosling, my college friends and I explored theory by yoking the serious to the silly, the obscure and the corny, the dense with the glib. We were cognizant that the world of perfect ideas shares an open border with the world of imperfect people—those who are impressed with their own cleverness, who meant to finish the reading between classes but maybe didn't

Hey girl.

Just thinking about Chandra Mohanty's theory that Western feminism problematically constructs the Third Wolrd woman as the pejorative "other"and the discursive colonial habits that keep women oppressed.

Me in 1998 (Courtesy http://feministryangosling.tumblr.com/)

get to it, or whose thinking isn't always motivated by what's above the neck. Sure, some people are interested in theory for the big ideas, the great learning, or the knowledge it promises; but like Feminist Ryan Gosling, my college friends and I were interested in theory for what we could do with it.

The following chapters elaborate some episodes from my youthful engagements with theory. But as with so many memorable activities, those engagements move in a few directions at once: you go somewhere, somewhere moves you, you step forward together. Along the way, I'll explain a little bit about what theory is, but the real objective of this short book is to explain some of how engaging with theory *feels*. Because I believe that feelings are best represented from the perspective of what it might be like to have them, the story will be peppered with anecdotes and tales and snippets from the youth I spent hungrily reading some really difficult books I mistook for the nourishment that they nonetheless became. All the things I'll tell you really happened, but what you're reading is not a memoir. Rather, anecdotes about myself are offered up as particular examples, in which I hope the reader will be able to better locate something more general.[*]

* * *

While there could arguably be an infinite number of feelings associated with theory, the ones dilated upon in what follows are some of those I associate with what academics like to call discipline—that is, with the experience of training for mastery in the terms and codes of a particular branch of knowledge. That process of discipline usually finds the energies that come with things like excitement, curiosity, and ambition in tension with those that come with other things like self-doubt, futility, and shame. It

[*]Though everything of what follows is to the best of my recollection true, in all cases nonpertinent details are omitted and the names of all nonpublic figures have been withheld; one story is condensed for narrative's sake from two separate experiences.

amounts, as I'll explain more in chapter 1, to a kind of thesis-antithesis narrative. For now, suffice it to say that though my contradictory feelings about theory owe a lot to my particular experiences (times, places, classes, teachers, lovers, friends, situations), the wager of this book is that similar feelings—similar pleasures and frustrations, similar contradictions—tend to crop up in experiences that are not mine at all.

Such, at least, is part of what we can see with Feminist Ryan Gosling. My college years were more than a decade gone when this meme first appeared, but the resonances between the way this meme and I attempted to project academic theory onto the world as we each found it support the idea that my feelings being disciplined by theory are far from unique. And while much of my initiation to theory happened at UC Santa Cruz, this particular location—and indeed many of the wonderful people I found there—nonetheless proves incidental to the larger claims I'm making about how theory feels. Had I been studying theory at any number of other colleges or universities—as friends hailing from Oberlin or Brown, Wesleyan or Iowa, Irvine or Swarthmore, all assure me—the outline of the story would be largely the same.

What couldn't entirely be changed without altering how theory felt to us isn't so much the place as the time. The fluorescence around ideas that runs through my story really became possible in the 1990s—at a particular moment in collegiate education in the United States, at a particular moment in the culture. Ours was not the theory of the Seventies, all phenomenology and structuralism, nor the theory of the Eighties, caught between deconstruction and Marxist feminism. Rather, theory in the Nineties was busy gathering an elite and increasingly canonical corps of French poststructuralism (often taught in these years for the first time as a required course for an undergraduate major like English or Comparative Literature) and spinning it headlong into the political fracas of the day: sex and AIDS and ACT UP; women of color feminism, black Marxism, the post-civil-rights generation and its many "firsts"; the end of the Cold War, the rethinking of the three worlds, nations and nationalism, decolonization; postmodernism in art, architecture, fashion, and film. In the Eighties, theory wrapped itself around academe, but in the Nineties, theory spilled out into the culture and the world. Or, to paraphrase Walter Benjamin, there is no document of theory in the Nineties that is not at the same time a document of the context of the Nineties.

It's that last point that the following chapters will stress. Yes, the process of learning about language, power, and history from a particular canon of theorists, and of imitating the singular idiolect in which they wrote, gave my friends and me a way of imagining our own lives and futures. But if it gave us a way of understanding something about the world, the world also gave us occasions for understanding theory. Along the way, we developed a rich sense and a robust language for understanding life as we found it and for how we were already living it out. The frequent battle cry of theory's detractors is "How does this apply to the real world?" It was clear to us even then that such detractors had missed the point.

The one important qualification that came to me in the years since I was in college, however, is that the real world has a way of changing. Contexts shift. If what follows is, according to the preceding outline, a story of Gen X, a story about what theory meant for those of us who got lost between the Boomers and the Millennials, it's at the same time an attempt to think through what theory might mean now that the Nineties are well over. A story driven by examples from reading theory *back then*, my narrative also considers latter-day instances (including memes like Feminist Ryan Gosling) in order to understand the extent to which "then" lives on now. Inasmuch as it does live on—inasmuch, in other words, as the present is always built on the past—my story attempts to look back in order to look forward. This is a book about reading theory in the Nineties for people who are reading theory now.

Individual chapters track five of the feelings that reading through, learning about, and living with theory made and make us feel: silly, stupid, sexy, seething, and stuck. Each chapter tells stories about its respective feeling as a way of elaborating the affective and intellectual work that theory did for me as a young person—and that, I'll wager, theory did for many of my peers and may still do for many more of its students. The five chapters roughly alternate between the lighter and the more serious aspects of being disciplined by theory.

Chapter 1, "Silly Theory," looks at the memes and jokes and goofball antics that move the high into the realm of the low. It takes seriously the scenes of humor and play where learning takes place, and it thinks about how missing the serious theoretical point of your reading can, all the same, be a way of arriving at an equally significant point.

Chapter 2, "Stupid Theory," reminds us that learning isn't all play and that one of the things that happens when people are confronted with intimidatingly abstract ideas is that they feel dumb. And resentful. This chapter underlines that one of theory's lessons is how to live with patience, how to handle something you don't understand.

Some things that we do not understand we still very much enjoy, and this possibility is the subject of chapter 3, "Sexy Theory." It looks at another ineluctable aspect of being young: how we learn to have preferences, how we begin to discriminate among love objects, and how one object becomes a way to love another.

Chapter 4, "Seething Theory," watches as love inevitably turns to rage, as debate and argument and even genuine fighting become ways we explore our attachments to ideas that feel anything but abstract. This chapter tracks some of the ways that the feelings we hold deep are and aren't ours—or, rather, how we learn to borrow anger and take on existing conflicts as a way to refine our own senses of the ideas and politics we care about.

Finally, chapter 5, "Stuck Theory," circles back to the problem of knowing versus doing, the question of how to put theory into practice. I stand by my convictions that reading theory in my youth was a way of being in the world and that the context of that world came to bear on theory. But that doesn't mean we solved it all, and it certainly doesn't mean that on the days not long after college when the Twin Towers fell, or when the United States invaded Iraq, theory could ever have been a big enough consolation or a powerful enough counterpoint to mendacious lies dressed up lethally as intelligence. Among the many things that happened on September 11, 2001, the Nineties finally, completely ended.

Avidly Reads Theory is not an introduction to theory. Many useful such guides exist, but you shouldn't have to consult them to appreciate the story I'm telling. All this story requires is a willingness to imagine how ideas have the power to become something more tangible and, I suppose, to imagine how it's possible to be so young and so foolhardy as to court life advice from schoolwork. What follows is a story about the emotional lives of ideas.

1

SILLY THEORY

Some years ago, I found myself at a twenty-four-hour vegetarian diner in a California college town, breakfasting with a dear friend. We had ordered coffee, but the main course was psychoanalysis. "You can't read Lacan without Hegel," I assured her earnestly. She broke into a grin, paused for a brief, dramatic moment, and then sang my words back to me, to the tune of Keith Richards and Mick Jagger's "You Can't Always Get What You Want," hitting the second syllable of "Hegel" in a flat F.

College brimmed with capital-T theory: that interdisciplinary set of literary and critical writings that blend Continental philosophy with qualitative sociology and theories of "the text." As generations of college students have noted, theory is often stylistically difficult and menacingly abstract, as obscure to the uninitiated as any other kind of heavy thinking, and yet way too cool to be called simply "philosophy." My friends and I were theory heads. We elected to read the Germanic sentences penned by

French absurdists, and we had a great time doing so. We were young and smug and deconstructed. In the classrooms and bookshops of fin-de-siècle California, we staked the foundation for our educations in an incisive critique of foundationalist thinking. We saw the irony, and we embraced it with the kind of reflexive detachment that today's fashionistas could only hope to conjure when they declare that something is "so Nineties."

Detached as it may have been, our experience of reading theory was far from dry. As the Jagger-cum-Lacan anecdote suggests, my college years embraced theory as though participating in what Lauren Berlant (in an essay I read over and over) called "a counter-politics of the silly object." We had a million puns (Kristeva? Whateva! Bourdieu? Bored me too! Understand deconstruction? You de Man!) We plotted the names of bands (Foucault's Hos, The Heidegrrrls) and cocktails (notably the Pink Freud, whose recipe I don't think we ever perfected but nearly all of whose iterations involved a banana). I wrote the treatment for a play called "Rendt: A Musical about AID," which replaced the transvestite character in Jonathan Larson's Broadway smash with a young, bohemian Hannah Arendt (also played by a transvestite). We created Lacanian drinking games for our favorite movies ("sip your Pink Freud when being and having are confused in a condition of lack"). And in perhaps my most starstruck celebrity sighting ever, I one day had the thrill of walking through a Longs Drugstore three paces behind Angela Davis, who (perhaps unaware of me, perhaps all too used to being followed) appeared to be doing nothing more revolutionary than buying cold medicine.

Playing silly games with serious ideas provided us with a way to lavish attention on the scene of our learning. It seems clear in retrospect that the actions of my college friends and me were not about theory, the object, but about creating a reflexive awareness of the context in which that object could (in fact did) circulate: through the space of early-morning diners and late-night parties, through the hands of amateur mixologists and bargain shoppers, and through the educational transformations of public school graduates into fledgling intellectuals. We aimed for some reciprocity between the serious things we were learning in school and rather less serious register in which we were living our lives outside of it.

It's in the same silly spirit that my students and their peers now turn highbrow theoretical ideas into goofy memes. Tired puns (advertisements for Freudian slippers) and doctored images (Friedrich Engels on the cover of "Cosmarxpolitan" magazine) occupy whole pages or feeds on platforms like Facebook, Tumblr, and Twitter. I read them with a burning sense of having missed out on their expansion into a visual domain of the kind of bad jokes that require a considerable education for one to earn the pleasure of finding them resoundingly stupid. Still, other contemporary attempts at silliness are more direct and more reminiscent of the jokes my friends and I made in college. Or, as a very bright young woman once wrote, unbidden, on her final exam for my intro theory course, "Your mama's so classless, she could be a Marxist utopia."

* * *

The grand alchemy for turning ideas into lives began, in my case, entirely inauspiciously. Introduction to Literary Theory was the only required class for my undergraduate major. It was offered every term, though the course varied by instructor, usually combining some elements of a survey—that is, some background in twentieth-century theories of language and representation—with emphasis on the particular professor's specialty. In the spring of my sophomore year, the professor happened to be a specialist in Russian modernism, and we spent half of the ten-week quarter studying theories of Russian formalism, which, for all their avant-garde provocation, had lost more than a little something in translation.

For the in-class midterm, our professor, straining for relevance to our contemporary situation, screened the video for the even-then-ignoble pop band Hanson's fourth single, "Weird," to be followed by an analytical essay in blue book. If this was an effort to connect theory to life, it faltered considerably. What I learned was, rather, an astonishing lesson in the coordination of formal and critical incoherence,

Hanson, "Weird," cover art for the Europe and UK single, 1998
(Courtesy Mercury Records)

because none of it made any sense. (The Hanson
brothers, whatever more generous interpreters might
find their merits to be, bear precious little on the theories of Viktor Shklovsky.) As pedagogical tragedies
go, it was ordinary enough. Though when the class
implausibly screened the very same benighted Hanson video again in the last week of the term, at the
behest of a guest lecturer who seemed not to know
we'd already been asked to view and analyze it, what
had once been tragedy was now clearly farce. It all

felt pretty silly, but not in a good way. If there was a lesson here, it had to do with how *not* to live.

The thing that piqued my interest that term had nothing to do with all these things we were focusing on. It was instead a reading sneaked into the sixth or seventh week, an essay by Jacques Derrida called "White Mythology." In what I now recognize as a classic of poststructuralist high theory, Derrida's sixty-page tour de force presents a rigorous deconstruction of the distinction between content and style in philosophical writing, showing how you can't have content without style and vice versa, how the two concepts fundamentally depend on each other, and ultimately going so far as to suggest that there is only a delusive difference between the language we use to represent reality and reality itself.

But I missed all that. I didn't walk away from the essay appreciating Derrida's critique of representation, which, arguably, is the whole point. What intrigued me, instead, was the operation of deconstruction. It fascinated me to think about dependence in Derrida's terms. Though generally unconcerned with how philosophical discourse worked, I was alive to the possibility that reality and the representation of reality depend on each other, such that reality is not meaningful without representation, and therefore that reality is not better than representation, for each constitutes the other.

My imagination moved from representation to infinity. All around me, conceptual hierarchies began to crumble. Men weren't better than women; humans weren't superior to animals; civilization was no better than barbarism. The arbitrariness of it all felt wild and enabling. Here was a use for the fin-de-siècle ennui that I spent the Nineties feeling anyway. Here was a version of the absurd and studied detachment that my friends and I cultivated during our off hours. Here was an account of the arbitrariness that I was pretty sure governed our world, but elevated and turned back on the world in a way that made the world as I found it a pretty silly place. Here was some justification that it really didn't matter whether you prioritized the authority of your teachers and their books or the dreams and longings of your peers. If you'd asked me as a college sophomore what "White Mythology" was about, I would probably, sincerely, have told you it was a manifesto for Revolution. My reading was a misreading, but what it lacked in precision it sure gained in verve. Here was a way to be.

It was not an accident, perhaps, that the scene of my seduction by theory was more or less extracurricular. Though "White Mythology" was on the syllabus, the class didn't much discuss it, and certainly not with the rigor that I now know it would require. On first reading, I didn't properly understand what I was reading and so was able to do that most magical thing that one sometimes does as a student or reader: I made it mean what I needed it to mean. This, I think, was one of the keys to "theory." To read rigorously, precisely, clearly—these things were among our aspirations, yet they were not what we as student readers usually accomplished. Instead, the imprecisions in our reading and learning were the story— they were a big part of what we meant by "theory." We were on a road toward abstract thinking, but the real fun was getting there. And we had a lot of fun.

* * *

Derrida's were not the only theories we were reading in college that had anticipated the possibility that we might get silly with serious ideas. Doing the opposite of what was intended with an idea was, at the least, a storied tradition for certain strains of critical thinking. I'm referring here to dialectics, that ancient mode of tripartite argument that reached its apex with German idealism and therefore remains associated for modern readers with Hegel and Marx. By definition, dialectical arguments have three steps: a *thesis*, wherein an idea is posited, an *antithesis*, wherein the thesis is negated, and a *synthesis*, wherein the contradictions between the thesis and the antithesis are suspended and blended into a new proposition. ("What's a Marxist?" asks an old joke. "Someone who can only count to three!") The second step, the antithetical move or dialectical negation, was best loved by twentieth-century Marxism, and it certainly jived with the ways that we irreverent theory heads wanted to negate the seriousness of theory and make it into something more fun.

At the time, however, we largely failed to make the connections between dialectical negation and just goofing. This failure back in the day surely had something to do with the day itself, as my college years fit squarely in that scant decade between the fall of the Berlin Wall in November 1989 and the fall of the Twin Towers on September 11, 2001. Between these two falls there came a glorious spring of optimism around globalization in both its economic and multicultural forms. These were victories for capitalism and, thereby, were understood as blows to the possibilities of actually existing socialism. Many Marxists doubled down and tried hard to rethink how human emancipation might look in an age that Susan Buck-Morss characterized as "the passing of mass utopia in east and west." Marxists, in other words, got more serious.

Not that they'd exactly been jokesters. In fact, few theorists of any persuasion were ever more legendarily serious than the famed Frankfurt School Marxist Theodor Adorno. He had been born the only child of a well-to-do German family in 1903, with a secular Jewish father and a Catholic mother. Adorno was her family name, and its original hyphenation to the patronymic—Wiesengrund-Adorno—was mutilated in the son's Nazi-fleeing application for US citizenship, rechristening him Theodor W. Adorno when he was already well into his thirties. The family name was far from the only thing Adorno lost in the war, but the episode rather neatly allegorizes the collapse of his turn-of-the-century idyllic upbringing when one realizes that the sacrificed name, Wiesengrund, literally means "meadow land." How could Adorno's mature thought be anything but marked by an almost fatal seriousness?

To add to the ignominy of having to seek exile for the offense of being only technically Jewish, Adorno had the complicated misfortune to end up in Pacific Palisades in the 1940s, down the coast from Malibu, where he could view the rise of capitalist techno-modernity from the belly of the Hollywood beast. His most famous exposition from the period is *Dialectic of Enlightenment*, a book of essays he coauthored with his friend, former teacher, and fellow émigré Max Horkheimer. It's core theoretical chapter, "The Culture Industry," distills in no uncertain terms how the industrial products of the postwar United States threaten human culture as we know it.

Culture, after all, is the shared activity of people, while industry is large-scale and profit-driven manufacturing. When culture becomes industry—when we buy recorded music instead of learning to play or when we pay for a movie ticket instead of escaping into our own reveries—we reside in a world where there is little difference between a rom-com and a bomb. Both, Adorno and Horkheimer argue, are industrial products fitted for mass consumption, designed to make money regardless of what they destroy. With a take-no-prisoners pessimism equaled only by the authors' rhetorical skill, "The Culture

Industry" manages to pack a whole dialectical argument into its three-word title.

Serious problems require serious solutions, yet the best shield Adorno and Horkheimer have against the machinations of the culture industry is to identify the problem, to name it, to expose it to view. Adorno and Horkheimer place faith in exposure. Though they stop short of saying so, their essay itself is about the only kind of resistance they can muster, insofar as the rarefied critical and philosophical writings of intellectuals do not, by design, accede to the level of mass appeal. And, as far as they are concerned, mass appeal has ruined just about everything else; or, in their own concluding words, even "personality scarcely signifies anything more than shining white teeth and freedom from body odor and emotions."

While Adorno and Horkheimer are not trying to be silly (witty, perhaps, but never silly), the wonderful pathos of juxtaposing BO and emotion, held in common by the fact that one might equally want to be free of each, is the kind of comparison one might expect from the likes not of a critic but of a comic, say an Amy Schumer (perhaps only coincidentally also a secular Jew whose comparatively idyllic early life was disrupted by major losses of wealth and prestige). Yet the temptation to smile or even laugh when reading a sentence like this from Adorno's corpus (and there are *lots* of them) has something to do with the fantastic accuracy of his diagnoses, which so successfully expose the pitfalls of capitalist techno-modernity. Adorno calls an unbearable world by its name, and we laugh not because we fail to believe him but because we believe him entirely. One of the functions of humor, after all, is to make bearable something that basically isn't or shouldn't be.

* * *

Had Adorno lived that long, he would perhaps have directed his truth-telling powers to elucidate how life in the Nineties became unbearable. Instead it has been largely in retrospect that other analysts came to see clearly the decade's patterns of economic redistribution, as dot-com and real estate booms made speculators rich, while welfare reforms and mass incarceration stripped many Americans of what remained of their social safety net. On the ground, however, the great indicator of trouble was the widespread cultivation of a certain attitude. When one left the house in the Nineties, it was not while sporting an Adornian faith in exposure but rather outfitted in the grand defensive armor of irony.

Irony was so everywhere in this decade that Alanis Morissette topped the charts in 1996 with a song called "Ironic" (which, ironically, had a patently incorrect definition of irony as its central conceit—you cannot make this up). Germane to our story, moreover, is the way that all this irony had a particularly blunting effect on the force of Marxist critique and, especially, on its faith in exposure. What could revealing the secret machinations of ideology possibly mean for people so *détaché* that they couldn't be shocked? Insights like Adorno's began to sound hollow in the ears of some more ironically attuned readers.

Looking at the Nineties through irony-colored glasses allowed us to feign boredom with the more unbearable aspects of the truths to which we were exposed. So, for example, when the button fell off a college friend's jacket, she joked about how they don't make child labor like they used to; or as people wondered about the safety of newly marketed gadgets like cell phones, my friends began to call them "brain cancer phones"; or again when a multiplex theater opened up opposite the independent local movie theater in our college town, we poked out of our ennui long enough to ask whether tonight we'd go to see a real movie or a corporate one. The examples sound trivial, juvenile, and a bit callous, and our irony was all of those things. Moreover, directing our irony (as in these actual examples from my youth) at economic and technological aspects of our globalizing world positioned irony neatly, if unintentionally, as a force opposed to Adornian exposure-based insight. We weren't critiquing the ascent of late capitalism; we were finding the language that would let us live in it.

Perhaps it was a function of coming of intellectual age in ironic times, but I never managed to identify myself as a Marxist. I was, nonetheless, very drawn to the writings of Marx and his inheritors, and for a couple of months in college I dreamed of writing a thesis that updated Marxism for the great age of irony. How can one place faith in exposure and the knowledge it yields, I wondered, if one lives in a world where everyone was ironic and detached and knew it all already? In the end, I abandoned the thesis because the question seemed too large. (And also because I could not read German and therefore could not engage with the likes of Adorno in the original. Powerlessness and pedantry can be passionate bedfellows.) Instead of writing that thesis, I just kept casually reading Marxist theory and tried to make peace with the fact that I would occasionally find it over-the-top and therefore a little funny.

Unbeknownst to college me, however, a related question had already been the subject of a UC Santa Cruz undergraduate thesis just a few years prior. Partially published in 1996 as "Capitalism and Schizophrenia: Contemporary Visual Culture and the Acceleration of Identity Formation/Dissolution" in the online journal *Negations*, Jonah Peretti's thesis argued that late capitalism, particularly by way of advertising, solicits a person's identifications and encourages them to form, dissolve, and re-form identities with great rapidity. The effect, he observes, is an acceleration in shopping, as the rate at which we consume tracks with the rates at which we attach ourselves to the objects with which we identify; but, he concludes, there is no reason "that radical groups could not use similar methods to challenge capitalism and develop alternative collective identities." Particularly prescient here is Peretti's sense that opting out of the psychological and aesthetic machinery of late capitalism—toward which Adorno and Horkheimer seem to aspire or along which we ironic Nineties intellectuals tried to skirt—was not the path. Instead, the only way out is through, and Peretti embraced rather than avoided. Ten years after he published his thesis, and coincidentally just months after I finished grad school and hit the unemployment line, Peretti put his theory into practice and founded a website to track viral media, which has since become Buzzfeed.

Perhaps theory prepared us for the memes after all.

Thesis: You can put serious things like theory into silly context

Media innovations like Buzzfeed and Twitter have left readers of theory in a world that increasingly measures messages in characters rather than paragraphs. Many media-literate (and especially younger) theory heads are ever more inclined to see that philosophical ideas can be pithy, aphoristic, and even pertinent to the kinds of banalities that swell social media feeds. Hence the existence of Chaka Lacan, whose name is a long-lived joke but whose short-lived Twitter persona (billed as "an interstitial space between hair mousse and the I") includes mashed-up gems from its two namesakes, like "Regarding this locus of the Other, of one sex as Other, what does this allow us to posit? I am every woman; it's all in me." Similarly and more prolifically, Kim Kierkegaardashian fuses the philosophy of Søren Kierkegaard with the tweets and observations of Kim Kardashian, to produce rather stunning pronouncements like "Because my dress isn't butt-tight, faith alone holds together the cleavages of existence." What's most astonishing about such a claim, of course, is that it illustrates Kardashian's outfit and Kierkegaard's input far more succinctly than either could explain for themselves. The ideas contained in these tweets matter, but they matter less than the medium of their expression. The ultimate context for these experiments is their form: theory isn't designed as a sound bite, but not because it couldn't be.

This lesson about context is not, however, one to which all people readily assent. Indeed, I have talked with some very smart folks who argue instead that an interest in acknowledging the scenes of theory's circulation is belittling—whether because it prioritizes context over text or because it forces lofty philosophical ideas to accommodate late-capitalist realism. Perhaps no meme is more likely to encourage such conclusions than Adorno Cats, a now-defunct Tumblr that pitilessly superimposes biting quotations from Adorno's critical writings onto color-enhanced photos of tiny kittens. It may be difficult not to look at a fluffy Siamese kitty captioned with "No emancipation without that of society"—the much-quoted conclusion to the 111th chapter of *Minima Moralia*

Dialectics (Courtesy adornocats.tumblr.com)

(whose proper topic, lest we forget, is Greek myth, sexism, and Hegel)—and not see a deliberate attempt to diffuse Adorno's dialectical critique in the over-large azure eyes of feline charm.

Such an interpretation, however, is decidedly un-Adornian. Ever alert to the machinations of ideology in minute locations, Adorno once devoted a substantial essay to his unbridled distaste for the *LA Times* horoscope columnist (an essay, I should confess, that I have never finished because every attempt at reading it leaves me laughing distractedly). Filling in the gap between culture and industry, the bland experience of individuals and the nefarious rationalizations of society, Adorno taught generations of thinkers to move fearlessly across seemingly disparate registers in order to expose the face of ideology—and there is no reason to suppose that he would make an exception when that face has whiskers. The cuteness of Adorno Cats, then, can be understood less as a bid for mastery over theory than as a complex embrace of theory's great dialectic of earnestness and silliness. Moreover, the cute, writes Sianne Ngai in a formidable kind of sequel to Adorno's aesthetic theory, is itself dialectical: something so diminutive invites us to imagine that we can control it, while also controlling us by provoking involuntary cooing. Only in our fantasies can mastery be a one-way street.

Antithesis: It's not context that makes theory silly but theory itself

Contrary to my previous proposition, examples like Chaka Lacan and Adorno Cats suggest that the currency of silliness in the vicinity of theory may have to do less with the uses to which theory can be put than with something that may inhere in theory itself. If that's true, then silliness is not an attempt to take theory down; rather, seriousness is an attempt to guard against the queer material of which theory is made— that big, difficult idea that always threatens to turn into a puddle of soft and ridiculous goo. The tonal seriousness and prosaic difficulty that characterizes theory's most celebrated practitioners and that is slavishly imitated by many zealous graduate students (including, as we will see in the next chapter, myself) is but a recent manifestation of the age-old paradox of trying to harness potential by denying its volatility. To secure themselves against volatility, serious practitioners of theory often become defensively prone toward obscure platitudes and dry clichés—toward a jargon-laden in-speak, in other words, that somewhere along the way forgot that any seriousness that studiously ignores unseriousness is rather hard to take seriously.

Quite in spite of any aspiration to seriousness on the part of its readers, theory's volatility persists. I cannot be the only person whose attempts to read Martin Heidegger have left me feeling like I am aboard the Hindenburg. I cannot be the only person who has giggled while reading Gilles Deleuze's unblinking analysis of Antonin Artaud's pronouncement that "All writing is PIG SHIT." I could not be the only student who was crippled with panic about what to wear to class on the day we were discussing Judith Butler's theories of gender performance. I know I am not the only person who has swooned while reading some of the more tender of Roland Barthes's caressing fragments on love.

Yet I freely admit my complicity with the silly movement of theory's dialectic, because, contra my more serious theoretical fam, I am not aware of any rule that says dialectics are most true when they tend toward the tragic. No less an authority on dialectical history than Marx himself posited that what appears once as tragedy appears a second time as farce. And, despite having lived at a time before the Hanson brothers appeared on anyone's theory midterm, Marx still knew that farce, properly executed, is pretty silly.

Synthesis: Silly theory and serious theory together make Theory

Acknowledging the silly in theory challenges not only the in-speakyness of theoretical jargon that takes theory too seriously but also the kind of demotic countersnobbery that dismisses theory out of hand for being too difficult. Those who are stationed irretrievably far into the antidifficulty camp tend to suppose that plain speech and realist genres count as neutral representations. The problem with this line of thinking is that the generic claims of normative realism, consequential though they may be, are little more than claims that representation ought to be banal. That is, the inverse of imagining that theory is too difficult tends to be imagining that what often counts as more basic is therefore more true, as though our culture's clichés—houses with white picket fences, politicians who tell it to you straight, beauty accentuated by its flaws, or career women who have it all—circulate in representation first and foremost because they really and unproblematically exist for some statistical majority. Instead, these clichés are as made up as Monique Wittig thought women's bodies were—which is to say, totally.

By this line of thinking, there is no objective reason why anyone should automatically understand the cuteness of a LOL Cat, any more or less than one should understand the thunderous exasperation of one of Adorno's monodies to the world that was cruelly sacrificed in war. Understanding either requires certain kinds of literacies that would enable you to recognize the idiom in which each operates. What's interesting, however, is that neither a theoretical bon mot nor a meme belongs exclusively to the domain of realism. Words like "realistic" or "normal" apply as little to *Minima Moralia* as they do to LOL Cats.

Moreover, I would argue that these words do not apply to these texts for what are in fact the same reasons: both texts are highly idiosyncratic appeals to general experience, both combine word and image to produce incongruous pictures of the everyday, both want something from reality that it contains primarily in fragments. To see only that each operates in a different idiom is, I would say, rather foolishly to misrecognize that both are trying to give voice to something that we readers of these texts have perhaps intuited but have heretofore been without a way to represent. Both begin with some familiar aspect of the world, and both use the recontextualizing arts of combination and juxtaposition to push off from what we think, toward what we have not yet thought.

The most valuable aspect of silliness, then, is that it works aslant both theory's aspirations to seriousness and realism's aspirations to referential simplicity. It reminds us that what is at stake in reading theory is not just what the theory says but also what we do with it—whether that means penning a devastating critique or downing a Pink Freud. In the act of mashing up Chaka Khan with Jacques Lacan, we're doing theory; but, more specifically, we're doing the work of making sense out of our less-than-theoretical world. The silliness of theory makes that work less urgent, though no less bracing. It enables readers of theory to relate theoretical ideas to the very world in which they encounter those ideas, to see how theory does and doesn't illuminate their realities, and to begin to put the pieces together. Here perhaps is the greatest lesson that theory can teach us about the world: some assembly is required. And who knows? It may be true that you can't read Lacan without Hegel. But if you try sometimes, you just might find, you get what you read.

2

STUPID THEORY

The warm-up years of college featured mostly twentieth-century theory, but by the time I arrived at the main stage of graduate school, the headliner was Immanuel Kant. His writings had never been entirely out of fashion, but they were finding wider audiences as the end of the Nineties yielded what was sometimes described as an "ethical turn" in criticism. Students of theory became interested in the likelihood that Kant's critical philosophy might be owed a debt by the French theories after 1968, which had, on the surface, rejected Kantian-style moralism and universalism in favor of a radical particularism. In 2000, with all the aura of an event, Verso Books brought out a volume called *Contingency, Hegemony, Universality: Contemporary Dialogues on the Left*, coauthored by Judith Butler, Ernesto Laclau, and Slavoj Žižek and in which, among other exchanges, Žižek accuses Butler of being a crypto-Kantian. Then, in 2001, I listened to a befrocked John Cameron Mitchell in *Hedwig and the Angry Inch* tell a fan how she'd been kicked out of university after delivering "a brilliant lecture on the aggressive influence of German philosophy on rock and roll entitled 'You,

Kant, Always Get What You Want.'" This last one was silly enough to make me feel that, maybe, Kant and I were going to get along.

We didn't. The problem was that reading Kant was not only not fun but also made me feel unusually stupid. I puzzled through *The Metaphysics of Morals* in one graduate course my first semester, through his *Anthropology* in another course the next, and through the *Critique of Practical Reason* during my second year. Trained by my very theoretical undergraduate education, I had absorbed the twentieth-century rejection of Kantian universalism without any precise appreciation for what was being rejected. Trying to catch up proved dizzying. Sitting on my blue Ikea couch, next to the stack of books that propped up my dream of postgraduate study, I could not, for the life of me, figure out why anyone should want to contemplate the nature of a "noumenon" "in itself." I was doing fine with Gilles Deleuze and John Locke and Giorgio Agamben and whatever else I'd been assigned that semester, but Kant threatened to be my Waterloo. Years later, I realized that my education had just been out of chronological sequence, that I'd adopted the antithesis before I'd learned the thesis. And even during that first semester of graduate school, I sensed dimly that I was missing some-such basic fact. But when the pieces eventually fell into place, learning what was missing did little to redeem those hours spent feeling really, genuinely, and totally stupid.

In retrospect, part of the problem was not just my scholarly context but Kant's. Or, rather, it was the flagrant fog of decontextualization that seemed to enshroud the study of Kant. We were assigned to read and discuss his ideas as if they were pure ideas: disembodied, ahistorical, undemonstrated. It was difficult to figure out why we had to read in this fog, and maybe we didn't have to so much as we just happened to. I now know that Kant would never deny that his writings belonged to history—to the time and the place and the man where they were incubated. But that acknowledgment of history certainly isn't the take-away of *The Metaphysics of Morals* or arguably of any of Kant's writings. Meanwhile, it turns out that their stylistic impenetrability can be understood in relation to the technical language of eighteenth-century German scholasticism, though such was not an observation anyone sitting with me around the seminar table ever uttered. I do remember being told that Kant followed the events of the French Revolution with great interest, but I found this contextual gesture more confusing than clarifying. What I knew of the French Revolution was barricades and guillotines, libertines and censors, wigs and hoop skirts. My trusted guide to the First Republic was the Marquis de Sade, and, by his standard, it seemed doubtful that Kant was following events of the same Revolution.

Without any context, I was flailing, reading paragraphs and passages over and over, until salvation came in the form for which one often hopes but doesn't dare to expect: late in *The Metaphysics of Morals*, Kant wrote a section about, of all things, butt-fucking. Here, finally, was something I understood.

The passage that fascinated me, in Mary Gregor's celebrated translation, reads in its entirety,

But it is not so easy to produce a rational proof that unnatural, and even merely unpurposive, use of one's sexual attribute is inadmissible as being a violation of duty to oneself (and indeed, as far as its unnatural use is concerned, a violation in the highest degree).—The *ground of proof* is, indeed, that by it man surrenders his personality (throwing it away), since he uses himself merely as a means to satisfy an animal impulse. But this does not explain the high degree of violation of the humanity in one's own person by such a vice in its unnaturalness, which seems in terms of its form (the disposition it involves) to exceed even murdering oneself. It consists, then, in this: that someone who defiantly casts off life as a burden is at least not making a feeble surrender to animal impulse in throwing himself away; murdering oneself requires courage, and in this disposition there is still always room for respect for the humanity in one's own person. But unnatural lust, which is complete abandonment of oneself to animal inclination, makes man not only an object of enjoyment but, still further, a thing that is contrary to nature, that is, a *loathsome* object, and so deprives him of all respect for himself.

Kant is trying to explain why "unnatural" sex is a morally bad thing. He admits it is a difficult point to prove but then asserts that proof is based in the fact that it is clearly bad. He follows up this apparent tautology with what I still cannot help but think of as a dick move, by contrasting unnatural sex unfavorably with suicide, because, hey, at least suicide requires courage.

If you do not accept the premise that unnatural sex is self-evidently bad, this "ground of proof" becomes obviously circular, and as someone who was having my share of unnatural sex and finding it not bad at all, I felt rather disinclined to give Kant the benefit of the doubt. Reading Kant was now my work, but I was not about to let my work infringe on my hobbies. How was *this* supposed to lead an ethical turn in criticism? Why did everybody in this brave new world of grad school like Kant so much, anyway? I decided I really didn't like him.

Somewhat more intellectually, I also began to wonder, if Kant's reasoning about unnatural sex was circular, how many other aspects of transcendental judgment were as well? It's a naive but not a totally bad question, and looking now at the paper I wrote that first semester of graduate school, I feel more embarrassment than stupidity. The paper is a textbook instance of beginner graduate-student work: a twenty-page essay driven by a big and basically worthwhile idea that suffers in execution from uneven development and insufficient awareness of relevant scholarly conversations, therefore obviously inventing the position the paper is trying to challenge. The writing is full of clumsy uses of jargon, some substantial digressions, and abrupt transitions. My syntax treats the verb "to be" like an MVP. The essay offered a spirited takedown, but I was picking on someone much too big for me. It hardly mattered that I had the inkling of a point.

Besides, nobody actually admired Kant for his brief discussions of sex. I didn't know it at the time, but they are quite famously bad. Kant once defined sex as "the reciprocal use that one human being makes of the sexual organs and capacities of another" and, whether because this was not unsexy enough or because he was (Kant was well into his seventies at the time of this publication in 1797), he followed this already-neutered turn of phrase with its Latin translation, "usus membrorum et facultatum sexualium alterius." Total boner kill. More than a century later, Walter Benjamin would skewer the "senile" philosopher by comparing his sterile definition of sex with the expressive longings of Mozart's contemporaneous *Marriage of Figaro* (1786). The tl;dr version of Benjamin's analysis was that Kant was doing it wrong. My point was the same, though I did not have the chops of a young Walter Benjamin and, more elementally, I really just had no idea what I was doing. Two decades after writing that paper, I still feel a little stupid that I didn't once know how little I knew about Kant.

* * *

Most people want to avoid feeling stupid, but academics take that avoidance to the extreme. We lean on our smarts for a sense of identity and (if we're lucky) for a paycheck. The exact measure of "smart" is hard to take, and few academics of my acquaintance have ever really tried. Back in grad school, my fellow students instead greeted our department's biweekly parade of distinguished visiting lecturers with ever more granular dissections and takedowns. We learned to explain in exquisite detail what was wrong with someone's argument or interpretation. But when something was good, our verbal acuity faltered. We could find an inexhaustible number of words for bad work, but we had just one word for good work. We called it "smart" and moved on quickly, afraid perhaps that a good idea or an impressive presentation would balance the scales that weighed seemingly bad scholarship so much more heavily than the good. Our smarts, so foundational to our developing sense of self, rested on how well we could explain that everyone else was a little stupid.

Elaborating other people's alleged stupidity and obfuscating their smarts is a singularly ungenerous way to be, and I don't recommend it. But in those days it was incredibly important not to feel stupid, which, by the way, it was even easier to feel. If you don't believe me, try sitting in a wood-paneled room full of professors and older graduate students, listening for forty-five consecutive minutes to a scholar monologue a paper (not just lecture but *actually read a script*) full of closely detailed and theoretically complex analysis of some novel or poem that you (and, judging by the liveliness of the Q&A, apparently you alone) have inexplicably managed to live twenty-three years of life and never before heard about, let alone read. So great was my growing anxiety about my own ignorance that I took to checking out from the library all the books by whoever was visiting campus that week and reading through them enough so that I might anticipate the scholar's method, if not also their argument. I never told anyone about this feat of what now seems like wild overpreparation because I was so full of shame that I hadn't already read everything.

In the middle of my third year of graduate school, sitting through a talk by a distinguished Victorianist, I felt the thrill of shock that immersion language students sometimes have, that, wait a minute, I can understand! As my friends and I whispered in the corridor on our way out of the building that night, I proudly announced that perhaps we had a hard time following the lecture not because of any failing on our part but because it just wasn't a very well-tuned analysis. I didn't get the conclusion because the lecture didn't support its conclusion. I wasn't stupid! The lecture was stupid! Regardless of whether that assessment was right, this newly ungenerous approach sure felt right—which is also to say that it felt insulating, self-protective.

When the person who came to speak was not just a literature professor, however, but a bona fide theorist, the tenor of the event was even more grandiose. My university was on the elite circuit through which some very influential theorists passed, and I have clear memories of lectures by Wendy Brown, Rey Chow, Lee Edelman, Eve Kosofsky Sedgwick, Hortense Spillers, Gayatri Spivak, and Michael Warner—what they said, how they spoke, what they wore. Many of these theorists lectured in the same rooms where any other departmental lecture was held, but during their talks the room felt different. People listened more attentively, and they asked questions more generously or more pointedly. Such was the mystique of theory that the person wielding it was taken to be offering something more than an interpretation with which you might simply disagree. We were literary scholars in training, and we were poised to challenge other literary scholars. They could be stupid, and we, like the theorists to whom we often deferred, could be smart.

* * *

Shame and stupidity are neighbors, but no fence separates their properties. For about two years between that first reading of *The Metaphysics of Morals* and my learning to follow an academic lecture in real time, I wrote and rewrote my first-semester seminar paper on Kant. With a doggedness that I barely understood, I stole time from my coursework and gave up months of my summers, dragging myself through Kant's three *Critiques* and reading secondary works about transcendental reason and the history of sexual regulation in late eighteenth-century Prussia. I learned the word "apodictic," which means something that is absolutely true and therefore beyond proof—the classic example is the existence of God. (Why is unnatural sex immoral? Apodictically speaking, it just is. You *definitely* do not have to try it to find out.) My simmering hate for this Kant guy whom everybody liked, and my desire to single-handedly prove that transcendental reason was circular, led me down the misguided path of what became my first real research project. At some level I was trying to prove that I understood Kant's ideas, but furiously doing that work also provoked person after person, teacher after classmate, to tell me, in more and less kinds ways, that I was being totally stupid.

Part of what felt maddening about this response was that, even in its gentler forms, it looked like an argument about context, some more eloquent version of "Things were different back then." Kant could not be expected to have a queer-positive take on sex, the objection ran, because there were no queer-positive takes on sex in Prussia in the 1790s. This last point is not strictly true (it depends on your historical interpretation), but what galled me was how easily it got Kant off the hook. He was trying to come up with a transcendental theory of morality grounded in human sense perception, and was it really such a big ask that he could maybe account for sexual variation? Reading Kant had made me feel stupid because the writings were so abstract and so decontextualized that I couldn't find a foothold. But when I did find a foothold, I was supposed to look past it because it didn't recognize Kant's historical context. It seemed that context only existed to protect decontextual reading.

While such an objection might be frustrating on its own terms, it was particularly frustrating to me, whose homosexuality felt rather like an urgent context for who I was and how I was trying to live. Six months before I started grad school, California's Prop. 22 had legally defined marriage as between one man and one woman—it was among the first of the redundant, state-level affirmations of the Federal Defense of Marriage Act, one of a large group of laws that would wind slowly toward the Supreme Court's legalization of gay marriage fifteen years later. The passage of Prop. 22 was also the outcome of an unabashedly homophobic campaign that nonetheless had been approved by more than sixty percent of voters. I left California for Maryland hoping for some mild refuge from this public hate-storm. So when I got there and found out that local hero Immanuel

Kant thought my unnatural sex life was also amoral, who can blame me for calling bullshit?

Greater minds than mine have been launched into academic careers by what more or less amounts to a vendetta. "I for my part have applied considerable time to understanding Hegelian philosophy and believe that I have understood it fairly well," complained Søren Kierkegaard in one of his first major publications. Yet he continues in shady understatement, "I am sufficiently brash to think that when I cannot understand particular passages despite all my pains, he himself may not have been entirely clear." What pleasure it would have given me at age twenty-four to have been so brazen as to claim something similar about Kant.

In the end, my stubborn pursuit of Kant never enabled me to throw down half so well as a young Kierkegaard, and undoubtedly what I really should have done was back away. It would have made much more sense, at least, to read something that supported what I was trying to do or who I was trying to be, instead of endlessly arguing with Kant. But I was drawn to the thing that made me feel stupid because I wanted to obliterate that feeling of stupidity through mastery. Who can blame me for that, either? My reaction to Kant was an overreaction, but it was one lodged deeply within the psychodrama of reading theory at an advanced level. Another thinker's thoughts provided the shell through which my own thoughts had to break, once they developed enough to stand on their own. In order to learn how to be a little more myself, I had to fill my head with a lot of someone else. It didn't matter that this someone else happened to be an antagonist.

* * *

Looking back now, I wonder, too, whether my grad-school friends and I enumerated the supposed stupidity of others for the same reasons that we shied away from explaining what was "smart": both were what our teachers taught us. It's pretty likely that these incredibly smart professors, whom we looked up to and relied on as mentors, were, in their own way, prone to feeling occasionally stupid. Now, as a professor myself, I certainly know from bad days, busy schedules, hasty prep periods, or canny student questions that I just can't answer on the fly. There's every reason to imagine that my professors prob-ably knew from these things too. But I say "probably" because I passed my student days ignorant of any such possibility. All I knew for sure was that my grad-school faculty pointed to our intellectual weak-nesses, and we accordingly learned to point to the weaknesses of others. I cannot say whether they were behaving defensively, pointing out our weaknesses in order to deflect any perception of theirs; but I am pretty certain our adoption of their behavior was, in its turn, a way to manage our own foibles.

Here, I realize, my experience may be far from universal. Many friends and acquaintances report that they earned graduate degrees from programs that encouraged all kinds of supportive and humane interlocution. So it bears emphasis that the point to this story doesn't fall with the defensive style of making others feel stupid (which, as I say, is mercifully not ubiquitous). Rather, the point is that one of the most central components of the way we learn is imitation. We do what our professors do.

Like so much other learning, university pedagogy proceeds by imitation. But this kind of imitation is fueled by something that bears a lot of structural similarities to hero worship. The challenge at the advanced level is that while you're figuring out how to be yourself in your academic context, you are more or less required to start behaving like someone else. Surely this structure is one of the big reasons for the abject aroma of graduate-student life. Few things are as likely to make you feel stupid as learning that you're being yourself wrong.

While imitation is a major force in university teaching, the question of whom one will imitate is open-ended. For some students, aspects of their identities, like gender or race or sexuality, account for the pull toward one professor rather than another. For others, it's an erotic frisson—a professor who plugs into the psychic space where, say, a parental figure fits. For others, it can be more apparently intellectual (a professor's specialty, a shared interest in some methodology), and plenty of times it's some mutual interest between professor and student, a dance of transference and countertransference whose variables are too multiple to name summarily. There's no formula for how to choose a hero, yet the constant in the whole experience is that you do (even, perhaps especially, when you say you refuse to).

The same is often true of the topics we study or the texts toward which we gravitate. How you feel about aspects of your social identity can affect your research, but so can all kinds of personal aesthetic concerns: for example, how you feel about tragedy or unrhymed couplets or strong female protagonists. No one who finds satisfaction in happy endings will want to write about, say, Frank Norris's novels, but someone who loves difficulty might spend upward of two aimless years writing diligently about Immanuel Kant. I hasten to add: someone who loves difficulty or who is trying to imitate the people who do.

Imitation isn't stupid, but it can make you do stupid things. In the case of Kant, I maintain that I wasn't stupid for failing to love someone whom everyone else loved. That was my truth, and truth, even of the sentimental variety, isn't stupid. But I was a complete and total fool for being so sure that it really was love that other people felt. I mean, some of my professors or fellow students may have been really into Kant's thought, but my graduate-school imitation game, at its core, had to with what we were reading, not, as I assumed, how we really felt about it.

The secret of my beginning years of graduate school is that I probably never would have read

Kant if my professors hadn't assigned his work. If my professors hadn't assigned it, surely my fellow students wouldn't have read it either; and it might have seemed like Kant wasn't that important, and I could have let things go. Conversely, had my college professors assigned me to read Kant, when I encountered his writings in graduate school, whatever else happened, I probably would not have so totally identified Kant with my postgraduate experience. He could have been another philosopher whom I read along the way, much as in those years I occasionally read texts by G. W. F. Hegel, Baruch Spinoza, or Friedrich Nietzsche. But, rightly or wrongly, my college professors didn't assign Kant and my grad-school professors did, and so Kant clicked into the place in the grad-school pantheon where I imagined heroes were represented. Since Kant wasn't a hero I wanted to worship, or a thinker I wanted to imitate, perversely, he became someone I had to take even more seriously.

Why did everybody in grad school like Kant so much? Maybe they didn't. But the imitation game can lead you to stupid conclusions. It took me years to prove and prove again to myself that reading something isn't an endorsement of it.

* * *

While the kinds of stupidity I've been describing cling like barnacles to all the stories of graduate education that I have ever heard or told, I admit that none of this, in and of itself, is caused by theory. Those who learn about theory in grad school may feel stupid in the face of it, but that stupidity just adds to the pile of stupidity that most grad students accumulate like so many unsubsidized loans. So I want to be completely clear about something: theory is not the primary thing that makes graduate students feel stupid; but, by corollary, when theory does make you feel stupid, it is so, so much worse than the ordinary stupid.

For the novice, reading theory often feels like reading an avant-garde literary work in translation. (Sometimes, in fact, it is *exactly* that.) For the novice who also made it as far as graduate school without encountering theory, the experience can be unmooring. It's easy enough to imagine feeling stupid when you have to learn how to be a professor by imitating one. (Like, hey, can't you just tell me what to do? Why do I have to watch and guess? What's going on here?) But the challenge levels up if you have no idea whom you're supposed to be imitating or to what end.

By analogy, suppose you've been assigned a novel to read—something you've never heard of, from a tradition with which you're unfamiliar. A person with prior experience reading novels can try to rely on the rules of genre to help make sense of the unfamiliar text. No doubt your appreciation of, say, a modern Chinese novel would expand if you could read it in the original language or if you'd read some of its contemporaries; but the basic fact that it's a novel will get you pretty far—as long as you have read some novels. If not, you'd be stuck. And if everyone else around you breezed through it, you'd feel not only stuck but stupid.

A friend tells the story of a discussion section for an English lecture class at an Ivy League university in the early Eighties. Her instructor brought to class his boom box and played a cassette recording of a recent lecture on campus by Jacques Derrida. The instructor sat back, arms folded with a hectoring nonchalance, and looked out at the bewildered students, who had no idea whom they were listening to or for what reason. It probably aided their comprehension very little that the recorded lecture happened to be in French.

Even at the top of the intellectual food chain, it seems, theory can make people feel stupid. Avital Ronell, in her book *Stupidity*, tells the story of meeting Paul de Man at a conference in Paris and trying to engage him in a discussion about Goethe. De Man observed that Goethe could be stupid, and as Ronell summarizes, "That could stop a girl in her tenure tracks. Not that I had a job at the time." Her first observation is wonderfully droll, but the second undercuts it with pathos. In hierarchal places like universities, where a lack of experience and a lack of status often track together, even a huge amount of theoretical reading and preparation can still be for naught.

During the summer that I slogged through Kant's *Critique of Pure Reason*, I learned that there were two versions: the "A" text, based on the first 1781 edition, and the "B" text, based on the substantial revisions to the second 1787 edition. After some research, I had purchased a translation that included both editions, but nothing in the book's scholarly apparatus made it clear to me which one I should read first or from which I should quote. Was the revision definitive? Did the original count more because it came first? I ultimately followed the convention I found in the secondary scholarship and cited both texts in the places where they overlapped, with in-text citations that looked something like "(A 207 / B 303)." I did so without any clear understanding of what was to be gained. My imitation felt like a thin front over my ignorance, and, as you can probably guess, doing it "right" didn't exactly make me feel smart.

* * *

I've already told you how theory didn't always make me feel stupid. The summer after college, with my graduate-school admission letter in hand and three months to kill, some friends and I found ourselves so enthusiastic about the sillier iterations of theory that we decided to have a reading group. Through some process of compromise or acclamation, we decided to read Benedict Anderson's *Imagined Communities*, Frantz Fanon's *Black Skin, White Masks*, Ann Stoler's *Race and the Education of Desire*, and Gayatri Spivak's *In Other Worlds*. We met regularly for vegan potluck dinners and discussion of these texts that represented to us a hole in our collective theoretical education that we called "postcolonial theory." For good measure, we called ourselves the PoCo Hos.

If these readings didn't make us feel stupid, that's not because they were easy. In fact, they were sophisticated, dense, learned, and full of references to places and contexts (Dutch colonial Indonesia, the French Antilles, British India) about which we were largely ignorant. It's also not the case that our readings were entirely sympathetic or friendly. I remember at least one raised-voices argument (in our discussion of the Stoler book, though I can't tell you what it was about—the emotions linger, but the content is gone). But the reason none of this ignorance or argument made anyone feel especially stupid had to do with the fact that the scene of our reading was extracurricular: it was dinner parties and friends. We cared very much about the politics of race and the decolonization of knowledge that our readings explored, but it was our luxury to care about them in a way that was playful, irreverent, haphazard—and, frankly, irresponsible. We were figuring out how to be ourselves in a scene of play, rather than a scene of work. We weren't imitating anyone.

In order to be smart, one doesn't have to feel stupid first, even if one often does feel it. Stupidity is one of the feelings that theory provokes, and in that, it should be understood not just as an individual experience but as a broader pattern. Stupidity in the face of theory is a structure of feeling. So is the smugness

I adopted as a graduate student. So too is the silliness I displayed as an undergrad. These structures of feeling, at their best, are just responses to one—and theory really is only one—of the endless things that life throws at you that doesn't make sense at first. The upshot of feeling stupid is that it can teach you something about the humility it takes to learn.

For the past dozen years, when nearly every year I have taught sections of an introductory literary theory class to undergraduate English and Comparative Literature majors, I try to reserve a few minutes at the beginning of each meeting for reactions. Students are invited to share raw emotions, unprocessed opinions; for five minutes, nothing they say has to have the dress or dignity of a point. Students' responses in this interval tend to be instructive in all kinds of ways, but the thing I most love is when someone will admit that the readings are difficult—especially when they really are, when, for example, we as a class are wading into Derrida's or Lacan's prose for the first time. I throw as much of my teacherly authority as I can into affirming this point. Yes, these readings are difficult. Yes, they can make you feel stupid. You are not alone in this. But now, let's figure out how to read it.

* * *

In my fourth year of graduate school, I polished up my paper on Kant and sent it off to an academic journal—my first attempt at scholarly publication. The essay had morphed into a theoretical investigation of deontological ethics as applied to the Todd Solondz film *Happiness*. My argument explored Kant's sense that morality can be evaluated based on universal rules and tested it against close readings of the film's brilliantly elliptical dialog between a serial sexual predator and his teenage son. Basically, I had written a Kantian ethics of child molesting. The journal sat with the essay for four long months and then wrote back and asked me if it was a joke. That was the word they used: "joke."

It turns out I wasn't stupid in the sense of being incapable; but I was awfully stupid in the sense of having been misguided. My years-long exercise of reading and writing about Kant turned out to be farcically pointless, which I might have known from the beginning if I'd just listened to all the people who told me so. I take some small comfort that, as stupidity goes, all that time spent learning too much about Kant barely registers in the grand scale of youthful folly. I tend to keep mum about it while friends swap stories from their freewheeling twenties about the mistakes they made with things like relationships or substance abuse. I don't think I deserve much credit for the fact that I was contemplating the nature of transcendental judgment while they were experimenting with lapses in theirs. It's small comfort that the thing all these experiences have in common is that we learned by doing them. I maintain that if my labor was misguided, it was not entirely meaningless. You can be stupid and also not be wrong.

* * *

A decade later, well after graduate school and even longer after I was done reading and writing about Kant, a filmmaker friend screened some of her work at the Museum of Modern Art in New York. Afterward, nearly the whole audience piled into a Hell's Kitchen bar to celebrate. It was past midnight on a humid summer weeknight, and the jubilant feeling of our friend's success made the air thicker still. I don't remember what exactly we cinephiles were chatting about in the line for drinks, but it had to do with something that someone described as self-evident. "It's apodictic," I volunteered. Into the uncomfortably loud silence my words had created, I tried to clarify: "It's a term that Kant uses." Silence. "To describe something that is true without being provable . . . like the existence of God." Their silence and stares fueled a mounting sense of terror at my faux pas. I recovered: "But I guess Kant knew better than to use it at a bar after midnight!"

They laughed, and conversation moved on. But I still bought the round of drinks.

3

SEXY THEORY

If Kant was the local hero of graduate school at the turn of the millennium, Michel Foucault was the patron saint of the Nineties liberal arts education. Kant we read abstractly, without attention to historical context; but Foucault encouraged us to think about the historical context for anything and everything. Whereas Kant, with his powdered wig and famously unvarying daily routine, was not very sexy, Foucault, with his bald pate and his leather jacket, was a walking, talking, thinking sexpot.

Part of Foucault's sex appeal had to do with the fact that he was more or less a contemporary. Someone like Kant or even Marx belonged to the ages, but Foucault had died only recently, in 1984. Granted, most people of my generation were neither old enough nor educated enough to have seriously studied his work by the time of his death, but that didn't change the fact that the separation between us and him was often no bigger than a single degree. Foucault spent a chunk of the early Eighties lecturing at Berkeley and visiting other US universities, where many of my professors had heard, met, or studied with him at one point or another. Plus, most of us in college in, say, 1997, had memories of 1984. Even if those memories were not *of* Foucault, they still made Foucault feel closer to us, proximate to the world we lived in.

The story of Foucault's visit to UC Santa Cruz went like this: he was in town for one speech only, and it was to be delivered in one of the large lecture halls on campus. He took to the stage and found his faculty hosts seated toward the front rows, with students and others farther back. Following the high-falutin academic style we Californians attributed to Foucault's native France, he lectured to those first rows, addressing his peers on the faculty. At some point during the talk, however, he looked up and caught the glance of a handsome graduate student. Foucault locked eyes with the young man, smiled, and then continued talking in the direction of the faculty. But he looked up again and held the student's gaze longer. And again, and even longer. By the end of the lecture, Foucault was speaking, with a smile on his face, only to the handsome graduate student in the back. Meanwhile, the handsome graduate student's very tall boyfriend had not failed to notice and was exhibiting defensive body language, putting his arm around his lover. It was told that the very tall boyfriend was following a course in Peace and Justice Studies, and so the event was shorthanded as "the time Foucault almost got beaten up by a seven-foot Quaker." In the overeager fashion I associate profoundly with my fledgling years in academia, the story's punch line was also the title.

I heard this story from one of my classmates, who was my age and so had definitely not been there. I repeat it, as I have over the years, without myself having been there. It is incredibly likely that all or part of this story is apocryphal. (I have, in fact, not been able to verify that Foucault ever visited UC Santa Cruz.) But who cares? The truth of the story is the clear impression it gives that Foucault was for us not only a living theorist but a particularly alive one. If being a student of theory required one to prostrate oneself before great thinkers, there was something incredibly pleasing in the idea that one of those great thinkers might make a dirty joke about prostration. We took Foucault to be that guy, and we loved him for it. Whether or not he was that guy, the fact that we needed him to be offers a useful reminder that desire and pleasure are part of the story of studying theory.

* * *

The first volume of Foucault's *The History of Sexuality* filled my time one summer day on the bus-to-train-to-ferry-to-bus trip between college and my parents' house. The reading was challenging but probably less so than my painfully self-conscious contemplation of what the strangers with whom I shared public transportation might see if they glanced in my direction. Half my time was spent looking at my book and the other half furtively glancing around to see if anyone was looking at me reading this book. I wondered what others might see in part because I had no definite sense, sitting there reading Foucault, what I was going for: gay? student? sophisticated reader of really difficult theory books? (My total lack of assurance about whether there was any overlap on that Venn diagram seems, in retrospect, sweet.) If my reading a book with "Sexuality" in the title conjured any intrigue, my fellow passengers managed to play their cards close. By the time I finished the fourth leg of my journey, I had to admit that no one appeared to have glanced in my direction.

If they had, however, it seemed pretty obvious to me that they should have recognized a book by Foucault as a gay book. All these years later, in a world where some public figures simply are gay, Foucault's out-and-queer-ness probably seems rather far from the most important thing about him. But you have to recall that in the Nineties there were no out gay news anchors or A-list actors or politicians or professional sports players. There was just one openly gay reality TV star, and he was the first functional gay adult whose story many Americans had ever gotten to know. In 1999, James Hormel began serving as the first openly gay person appointed as a US ambassador, and if you have any doubts that the controversial nature of his appointment had to do with the national mainstreaming of homophobia in those years, recall that his post was to nowhere more diplomatically significant than Luxembourg.

Such a world, needless to say, made little room for out gay philosophers. And so because in the Nineties, on the one hand, Foucault's writings were having an impact on nearly every discipline of study in the humanities and social sciences and, on the other, the people who got to have an impact were rarely gay, Foucault's gayness loomed, symbolic and large. It felt, to use a Foucauldian word, political, and the politics of this knowledge framed how many of us thought about Foucault. At the same time, that frame did little to explain his theories, and, indeed, there is a real extent to which Foucault mistrusted the political value placed on biographical facts for theoretical interpretation. He wasn't wrong to do so.

After Foucault died in 1984, three biographies appeared in short order: Didier Eribon's *Michel Foucault* (1989; translated into English in 1991), David Macey's *The Lives of Michel Foucault* (1993), and James Miller's *The Passion of Michel Foucault* (1993). All three discussed Foucault's homosexuality and its impact on his life and thought, albeit to very different ends. Eribon did so affirmatively but guardedly (though, written from within a particularly AIDS-phobic moment in French culture, courageously), and Macey did so frankly, matter-of-factly, as though homosexuality simply numbered among a biographer's challenges for empirical reconstruction. Miller, however, did so with moments of undisguised prurience toward the queer worlds that his narrative exposed to the light of the heteronormative day. Published shortly thereafter, David Halperin's *Saint Foucault* (1995) raced in with a rebuttal to Miller's biography, as lengthy as it was scathing, detailing the ways that Foucault's aversion to the biographical fallacy was precisely an aversion to the kinds of homophobic discreditation that Miller so gamely advanced.

Many of my fellow college students admired Halperin's book, meaning, among other things, that it must have shown up on a number of different syllabi in those years. (I didn't read it for class but instead because a cute boy wanted me to.) I too admired the book, but my thinking about the authors I was reading nonetheless inclined toward their biographies. I *wanted* a gay Foucault. I was glad I had one, and I didn't want to have to give him up in the name of theoretical consistency.

Eribon, at some level, wanted a gay Foucault too. Of the three biographers, he was the one who had been Foucault's friend, and he justified his biography by arguing that Foucault was, on his own terms, an author: the words Foucault penned begot a discourse whose scope proved to be far larger than the writings themselves. In this way, Eribon anticipated by more than two decades the finest exposition of Foucault's notion of the author-function, Beyoncé's 2016 claim "You know you that bitch when you cause all this conversation." Yet in those long-ago days when Beyoncé contended only in grade-school talent shows, Eribon already saw, correctly, that Foucault was "that bitch." So he split the difference and wrote a book whose subject was the genesis of Foucault's impact, as much as a study of his life. The result is a respectful and measured biography of a public figure who required a lot of privacy. Though admirable as an intellectual accomplishment, Eribon's story also disappointed. As is the case with so many love triangles, I just wanted more of Foucault than Eribon felt he could allow me.

And so, though Foucault probably had my strongest theoretical allegiance in those days, when it came to thinking about biography, I was drawn much more toward deconstruction. Jacques Derrida, for example, advanced the notion of the "signature," according to which all texts we write or create, by virtue of having been written or created by us, obliquely stand in for us—and therefore are to some extent about us as much as they are about their nominal topics. Paul de Man made a related claim in his bravura late essay "Autobiography as De-facement," imagining that all writing is autobiographical but, for the same reason, all autobiography is merely writing. Deconstruction, in other words, along with my laxity for logical consistency and my eclectic reading habits, got me around the part where reading Foucault because of some detail in his biography bordered on misreading Foucault.

It's tempting to imagine, however, that what deconstruction says about writing is also true of reading. Did my eclectic reading habits, willfully mixing up different schemata and theoretical discourses, amount somehow to my own signature, my own way of finding words, not just for representation and power and history but also for myself? A sympathetic interpretation of the story of my attempt to read Foucault on public transit might point in that direction. Whatever else I may have learned from *The History of Sexuality* (actually, quite a lot), I was reading it that day on the bus, train, and ferry *because* it seemed to me like a gay book and, in the act of reading a gay book, I wanted to see how I myself might be read.

One of my recurrent jokes in those less-than-surefooted years was that my sexual orientation was theoretical. It wasn't funny, as jokes go, or strictly true, but it got two things right. First, it named the way that theory, for me as a student, was a libidinal object, something in which my investments were not purely intellectual; and second, it pointed to the ways that sexual orientation—the part of who we are that depends on what we're drawn toward—is defined not just by the reality of how our needs get satisfied but equally by the aspirational horizons of our desires.

Desire is part of the scene of reading theory, and desire is unruly. One doesn't always want what one should, and one reads texts with fidelity to one's own wants as much as (sometimes more than) to whatever the texts themselves happen to claim. What aligned my desire for Foucault's text into the approximate shape of a sexual desire, I think, has something to do with the tentativeness of my reading in order to be read. This desire was not the self-consciousness that Hegel describes with that term or the will-to-power that Nietzsche designates; "desire" in this context had much more the character of Freud's ambivalent eroticism: I wanted but hardly knew what I wanted. My reading engaged in an experiment with seeing where some part of me could go, with how it felt to be or be found in a place toward which my fantasies (of who I might be, of how I might be seen) tugged me along. I started reading Foucault's book with no idea how it would end.

* * *

Everyone's sexual orientation in the Nineties couldn't help but be a bit theoretical, and the AIDS crisis was the culprit. Sexually transmitted infections were hardly new; but suddenly one was widespread and fatal, and the people who were dying in the largest numbers were often young enough to be new to sex. At the same time, the slow and uneven public response to the epidemic signaled how aggressively the conservative Eighties were lashing back against the free-love Seventies. (At the time, we called them the Sixties, but the dates don't check out; when people talked about "the Sixties," they often meant something like 1967–1977—roughly, the Summer of Love to the Iranian Revolution.) In this context, sex became, to say the least, a bit complicated.

AIDS scrambled the available narratives around sex, making sex something that nearly everyone had to sort out in the abstract. Reports from the early days of the epidemic indicated that the HIV infection was (1) sexually transmitted and (2) prevalent among gay men. Just these two facts meant that all kinds of people, from educators to public health professionals to politicians to family members, suddenly had to confront the mechanics of gay male sex. It was a singular feature of the early Nineties that one could watch the nightly news and listen to segments in which correspondents and experts had a dressed-up version of a locker-room conversation: does this or that activity "count" as sex? Similarly, condoms were an ineluctable part of sex in the Nineties, and I understood in principle which kinds of situations did and did not require them years before I would have any occasion to use one myself.

The midst of the AIDS crisis was an unfortunate time to hit puberty, because it meant that one began to approach one's own sex life at a moment when the cultural meanings for sex were under unbearable pressure. Even friends my age who were never queer or protoqueer report that in adolescence sex often seemed much more scary than fun. Well before we'd experienced its pleasures, we were confronted with the fact that sex was potentially lethal. Such a possibility amplified the already guilt-prone feelings of puberty, forcing desire to live in extra-cramped quarters with embarrassment. The AIDS crisis, as Simon Watney summed up in 1987, was not only a public health crisis, but "it involves a crisis of representation itself, a crisis over the entire framing of knowledge about the human body and its capacities for sexual pleasure." Those of us a bit younger than Watney came of age in a world where love felt really, really far from free.

The small silver lining attending this scrambling of prior generations' narratives about sex was the chance it provided to make new narratives. By the time I got to college, there were a good number of examples: Audre Lorde arguing that the erotic was a source of political as well as personal power or Douglas Crimp suggesting that safer sex practices showcased the resourcefulness of queers in a homophobic world or Gloria Anzaldúa sorting out the jumbled ways that sexuality gets lived in relation to gender, race, religion, and geography. I was particularly moved when I watched Marlon Riggs's experimental film *Tongues Untied*, which introduced me to Essex Hemphill's poetry and, especially, the incantatory line "Now we think / As we fuck," where "as" means *like* but also *while*. My all-time favorite text from that period is Cheryl Dunye's film *The Watermelon Woman*, an early contribution to the "mockumentary" genre, in which a black butch lesbian aspiring filmmaker in an interracial relationship pieces together—from scrapbooks, chance interviews, and the credit reels of old Hollywood movies—the story of a black butch lesbian aspiring actor in an interracial relationship. Sometimes, the film tells us, you have to create your own history.

All of these texts thought beautifully, boldly, and abstractly about sex and its place in a broader world. Accordingly, these texts looked to us like theory, and we ranked them with and read them alongside other so-called high theorists like Derrida and Adorno. It was clear to me even as a college student that such an assessment was not universal; I was well aware that a proper philosophy class would favor Locke's theory of personhood over Lorde's. But it was equally clear to me in those years that the connections between philosophy and theory and just thinking abstractly about social life were connections that I was not alone in needing to make.

* * *

Less than ten minutes from the end of Kirby Dick and Amy Ziering Kofman's feature-length 2002 documentary *Derrida*, the great philosopher is asked what he would want to see in a documentary about a great philosopher like Kant, Heidegger, or Hegel. After a thoughtful pause that lasts an uncomfortable twelve seconds, Derrida replies, "Their sex lives." I don't mean a porno, he clarifies, but to hear them talk about their sex lives would be interesting because it is the thing they refuse to talk about. Why, he asks, turning what is already meta-question around again, do philosophers present their thoughts as though they, the people who think those thoughts, are asexual?

Why, indeed. The film introduces us to Derrida's wife, Marguerite, but omits any acknowledgment of

the affair and son he had with the philosopher Sylvi-
ane Agacinski. Meanwhile, despite a volatile and, one
would not have to go far out on a limb to say, libidinal teacher-student dynamic between the two men,
Derrida never so much as mentions Foucault's name.

* * *

After the publication of the first volume of *The History of Sexuality* in 1976, Foucault did not publish
a single-author book until he was on his deathbed
in 1984. In those nearly eight years, he taught and
researched and changed his mind about what made
up the history of sexuality. He addresses the generative quality of this delay in the preface to the second
volume, *The Use of Pleasure*, with an unusual degree
of writerly clarity: "to those, in short, for whom to
work in the midst of uncertainty and apprehension is
tantamount to failure, all I can say is that clearly we
are not from the same planet." I admit I would have
to strain to find this moment outright sexy, but I am
more than a little attracted to its confidence.

So much of the work that's associated with these
last eight years of Foucault's life takes the form of
seminars and interviews, the latter of which he increasingly granted to the gay press both in France
and in the United States. His doing so required a del-
icate touch, as Foucault clearly wanted to encourage
the flourishing of gay expression that the gay press
represented, but he also maintained his skepticism
about why, among all aspects of what makes up a

person, sexuality was so privileged as to appear to tell the truth of one's self. In a 1981 interview with the recently founded *Le gai pied*, Foucault pushes the point, responding to an interviewer's question about whether desire is dependent on age by pivoting away from desire at all. He speaks of homosexuality not as a form of desire or even as a sexual practice but as a social relationship:

> One of the concessions one makes to others is not to present homosexuality as anything but a kind of immediate pleasure, of two young men meeting in the street, seducing each other with a look, grabbing each other's asses and getting each other off in a quarter of an hour. There you have a kind of neat image of homosexuality without any possibility of generating unease, and for two reasons: it responds to a reassuring canon of beauty, and it cancels everything that can be troubling in affection, tenderness, friendship, fidelity, camaraderie, and companionship, things that our rather sanitized society can't allow a place for without fearing the formation of new alliances and the tying together of unforeseen lines of force. I think that's what makes homosexuality "disturbing": the homosexual mode of life, much more than the sexual act itself. To imagine a sexual act that doesn't conform to law or nature is not what disturbs people. But that individuals are beginning to love one another—there's the problem.

It's difficult to put my finger on a story or an example of how consequential these sentences felt, because they were infused almost completely into the ways that my friends and I imagined sexuality. AIDS had given us a sense that the narrative we had inherited about sex was broken, but a framework like Foucault's helped us to imagine that friendship could be one of the side benefits of sex, rather than the other way around—that sex might exist in new kinds of relations, that it could be the basis of something whose shape we could not yet see. Fatality yielded to possibility, and it made a wonderful addendum that this interview had been translated into English and published with the title "Friendship as a Way of Life." Some new way of living was exactly what we dreamed of forging out of sex.

However, we were also reading in the ways our desires pulled. To be sure, if Foucault was generative in his account of sexuality as sociability, he was nonetheless critical of sexuality as individual psychology and identity. We followed him one way more than the other. I'm certain that it felt important to my friends and classmates in college that we had the chance to be ourselves, and the idiom of sexuality—desire, fantasy, and the specification of identity—was undoubtedly something that, to us, felt true, in all the ways that Foucault critiques. Coming out as gay (or bi or queer or whatever else) was a potent political idiom in the Nineties, one that had arguably gained more clout in the ten years after Foucault's death than in the ten before.

The saving grace of the situation, however, was that the conversation did not end there. Really, it barely began there. Coming out seemed to us to be the springboard not for finding ourselves but for finding one another. It was a one-way ticket to getting to make up a social world however you might want it to look: creating history but also creating a present and future. There could be affection, tenderness, friendship, fidelity, camaraderie, and companionship, and these things could be coextensive with sex or not. Whether you were lovers with someone was something we learned to value but also to place on a spectrum with other dimensions of friendship. These ideas inflated to the lofty status of an ethic. We wanted to have sex, and we wanted to have a way of life; and we relished the support that theory lent to the idea that these wants overlapped significantly. Sex grew intelligible with theory, and from that vantage theory looked pretty sexy.

Take gay marriage, for example. Already in the mid-1990s the issue was being debated at the state level, including high-profile cases in Hawaii and Massachusetts. But these had for us little of the aura of a meaningful civil rights issue. We young people in our queer relationships imagined instead that we were engaged in forms of social attachment that were genuinely alternative to marriage, that, indeed, might be better than marriage, and that in any case deserved to be tested out.

Test takers abounded. I knew people who were polyamorous, with multiple serious partners at once, or people who only dated couples, effectively having a relationship with other people's relationships. I met people who were best friends and sometimes even roommates with their exes—a testament to the ways that connections endure even if romance doesn't work out. I knew other people in fairly conventional, monogamous partnerships who nonetheless cohabitated well into adulthood with other individuals or couples—chosen family—and shared meals and bills and raised children and, sometimes, buried one another. All of these were attempts to test how life might be lived, various schemes for mapping affection and attachment and responsibility otherwise than in the normative monogamous, couple-based pattern that, to many of us who'd grown up in a world of women wage earners and no-fault divorce, looked fairly arbitrary. By comparison, gay marriage seemed like a retrograde position.

Amid all this experimentation, perhaps the story that best illustrates the reach of "Friendship as a Way of Life" into the ethos of my youth is the one in which, in about 2010, a decade after college and well into my first teaching job, I sat down to reread the interview and was shocked to discovered that I'd never read it before. Parts of it were completely familiar, and I must have encountered them in excerpt or citation. But most of it was just brand new. Meanwhile, nowhere among my books or papers was there even a copy of the interview to be found. When I Googled further, it became clear that the interview had been published only in books I was quite sure I'd never owned. Though I had memories and impressions of "Friendship as a Way of Life," I had no distinct memory of reading it. All the same, it felt consistent with the spirit of the piece to imagine that I'd put the practice of making a life ahead of reading the theory.

* * *

Foucault theorized sexuality, but he also lived it out. This duality was confirmed in conjunction with his early visits to Berkeley in 1975 and again in 1979 and after. One consequence—let's call it the theoretical or at least professional one—was that two Berkeley professors, Hubert Dreyfus and Paul Rabinow, began to collaborate with Foucault on an authoritative primer to his thought, eventually published as *Michel Foucault: Beyond Structuralism and Hermeneutics* (1982); but another consequence—let's call it the living or perhaps personal one—was that a Claremont College professor, Simeon Wade, and his lover, Michael Stoneman, invited Foucault to join them for an LSD trip in Death Valley, involving as well an interview, which Wade self-published as part of a zine called *Chez Foucault* in 1978, and an account of the LSD trip, *Michel Foucault in Death Valley*, published only in 2019, that a number of Foucault scholars and biographers have worked hard to track down.

II. The Countersciences which explore the Unconscious (the Unthought), the conditions which make life, language, labor and thought possible

    (1) psychoanalysis which burrows into the individual unconscious by means of transference (talk, projection, bioenergetics, tableau) between analyst and patient in order to free us from

        (a) obsessions, by showing how and when we lost the object of our desire thereby liberating us to find new objects of desire

        (b) the fear of death, by revealing to us that we will in fact die one day, thereby releasing us from the night of the living dead

    (2) ethnology (cultural anthropology) which penetrates the social unconscious by deciphering the structures and conditions which make possible myths (collective hallucinations) and social relationships (the great ethnologist Levi-Strauss maintains that ethnology dissolves man)

    (3) the archeology of knowledge, which uncovers the unconscious network of rules and regularities creating discursive formations

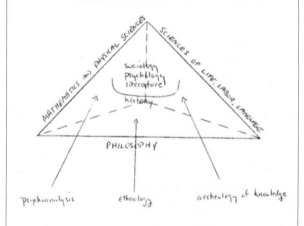

Methodology, from *Chez Foucault* (1978)

According to the kind of academic perspective from which theory is usually studied, it's easy enough to imagine that the work with Dreyfus and Rabinow is Foucault's real work and that his time with Wade and Stoneman was a diversion. The mechanisms of academic knowledge transmission (what gets recorded, what gets published, what qualifies a person for tenure) would seem to reinforce the point—as, by the way, do Foucault's biographers (and if you don't believe me, check which proper names get indexed). But such a point pulls as much against Foucault's corpus of thought as it does away from the facts of his biography. There is absolutely no indication that Foucault, the guy who once argued that Nietzsche's grocery list might properly be included among Nietzsche's complete works, would posit any meaningful difference between the professional collaborations of the mind and the improvisational collaborations of the flesh.

In the same spirit, fifteen years after Wade's Foucault zine, in 1993, Andrea Lawlor anonymously published a fanzine called *Judy!* It presents a loving, irreverent, and unmistakably erotic tribute to Judith Butler, author of the foundational (and then quite recent) theoretical tomes *Gender Trouble* (1990) and *Bodies That Matter* (1993). Lawlor was a college student in Iowa at the time, and the zine tells of a pilgrimage to an MLA conference in New York City, where she met or hoped to meet Butler (the zine is elliptical on the juicier details). Unable to find many pictures of Butler in those pre-Google days, she festooned the zine with other Judys, most prominently Judy Garland, as well as with cheeky and out-of-context references to Butlerian concepts like the lesbian phallus (which, isolated from the complicated theoretical armature that Butler's chapter on this topic elaborates, sounds undeniably like a sex toy—a really hot sex toy). Coordinating the work of the mind and the work of the body were part of Butler's project, as they had been for Foucault, as it seems they were for Wade and Lawlor in turn. In all these cases, as most certainly in my own, reading theory involved the dual experience of reading about gender and sexuality, on the one hand, and trying to navigate the fact of having a gender and a sexuality, on the other.

The broader project of trying to relate these theories and practices in the Nineties blossomed under the sign of "queer theory." Many of its practitioners were literature scholars, lots of whom were the products of elite graduate programs but who had also earned their stripes in the women's movement, in AIDS activism, and/or in antiracist political organizing. After about 1991, their common project came to be called queer theory, though the phrase is noticeably absent from books by Foucault, Butler, or Eve Kosofsky Sedgwick that are often taken as foundational to the movement. Queer theory looked most often in those early days like an offshoot of radical feminism that wanted to proceed from a critique

LOCATION: MAIN
COMMANDS:
V   View Record
F   Forward
N   Next Record
P   Previous Record
I   Index
H   Held
O   Other Options

Search Request: K=BUTCH
ILSON RECORD -- 7 of 14 Entries Found
--- Screen 1 of 1 -------------

"I felt alienation because they were
dancing around to women's music
and I really couldn't stand it," -Judy in
Artforum November 1992

Search Request: A=BUTLER, JUDITH
Search Results: 13 Entries Found

BUTLER JUDITH
1   DE... A...C...N IN S...RE SAINT GENE
2   FOU CAU...ND...E PARADOX OF BODI INSCRIPTI
3   KNOWING ...D HISTORY BOOK REVIEW PPROPRIATIO
4   KNOWING AND HISTORY REVIEW ARTICLE <1990> (
5   PERFORM...IVE ...CTS AND GENDER CONSTITUTION AN
6   ...EX AND GENDER IN ...MON DE BEAUVOIRS ...COND
7   SPIRIT IN ASHES ...OK RE...EW ...EGE HEIDEGGER
8   SPIRIT IN ASHES REVIEW ARTICLE <1988> (HU)

BUTLER JUDITH P
...E...TROUBLE BOOK REVIEW ...EMIN...SM AND THE
...TE...BLE BOOK REVIEW ...EMIN... AN
...U...S...T BOOK REVIEW ... R...I

DON'T BE AMENDED
READ JUDY

Judy! zine, page 20 (Courtesy Andrea Lawlor)

of the idea that sex and gender had any basis in nature (that sex itself and not just gender was, in the resident vernacular, "socially constructed"). Queer theorists, then, were people who knew something about the relationship between theory and practice, and queer theory became a kind of road map for those of us who wanted to better understand their relationship.

I don't mean to make queer theory sound as though its project were entirely coterminous with that of, say, self-help literature. But I would insist that queer theory was trying to think about the cultural, political, and personal meanings of sex at a moment in the Nineties when those meanings were more up for grabs than they had been in at least a generation. Whether queer theory was a cause or effect of that historical epoch, I cannot finally say. (I mean: both.) Nevertheless, something about that moment meant that queer theory's work of sorting out what sex means and the more broad-based work among theorists of relating the mind to the body felt very obviously like related tasks.

For example, one of most enduringly generative theory texts of the Nineties remains Sedgwick's *Epistemology of the Closet* (1990), and among its many excellent concepts is "gender transitivity." Against the idea that one's biological sex (let's say, male) would line up with one's gender presentation (masculine) and one's fantasy life (dominant) and one's preferred sexual object (women)—a view she summarized as "gender separatist" but what we might now call "het-ero-" or "cis-normative"—Sedgwick theorized that a person might experience all kinds of misalignments in this scheme. Homosexuality, in which the gender of one's preferred sexual object is not normatively optimized with other components of identity, was, for her, just one of many complications. An intriguing consequence of this scheme was that a person might have a gender and a preferred sexual object that all lined up with her or his biological sex while nonetheless maintaining a fantasy life that veered elsewhere. That possibility was a queerness, just as much as any more observable social behavior like homoerotic sex or gender nonconformity.

The excitement of such a possibility had to do with the implication that queerness wasn't just a matter of sexual identity in the usual sense. Gender transitivity could happen at the level of fantasy, and fantasies could get acted out or not. Queer theory in this vein did a lot to validate the possibility that you might desire the idea of something you didn't actually want to do or that you might identify with people who were not in some observable ways "like" you. Queer theory dignified the prospect that you could see yourself as someone at variance from what other people see about you. At the same time, those possibilities didn't make you a particular kind of person, not an x or a type or kind, unless perhaps you wanted to be. "Queer" held open the space of something astonishingly variable and open-ended. All you had to be was yourself, in all your myriad social, psychological, and performative complexity.

Accordingly, I recall a large number of conversations in those years with people who were functionally speaking gay men—assigned male at birth, chose other men as their preferred sexual objects—who identified heavily with lesbians. Playful, sometimes flirtatious affinities between gay men and lesbians all landed along the spectrum of "queer," though whether those landings properly snapped identity into place or into flux depended on other variables like your community, its politics, its average age.

But again I don't mean to make queer theory sound purely intellectual. The summer I read *Epistemology of the Closet* I did so mostly on the bus, commuting between the beautiful campus up on a tree-covered hill where I worked and the dumpy condo down by the low-rent beach in the unincorporated part of town where I lived. I'd fill my head with Sedgwick's abstract ideas about how the hetero/homo dichotomy was central to knowledge production in the modern West more generally and then get home, change into my running shoes, and think it through as I ran along the road by the beach. One day my running path veered closer to the beach parking lot, where I saw a pair of muscly surfers stripping off their wet suits in the showers. Suddenly few things in the world seemed to have the complexity of a dichotomy. I ran on, aroused and embarrassed by the body's intrusion into the contemplation of the mind.

It honestly did not occur to me that I might have asked those guys to join my reading group.

* * *

Part of all this interest in transitivity had to do with the fact that so much of sex in the Nineties was consigned to the realm of fantasy. In a 1982 interview, later published in the *Advocate*, Foucault gets asked what he thinks about the proliferation of "male homosexual practices" in the past ten years: "porn movies, clubs for S&M or fistfucking, and so forth." Once again steering the conversation away from the idea that desire is innate, Foucault replies that it's not that people always wanted to participate in S/M scenes so much as that the availability of those scenes becomes a place where people can learn and desire in new ways. Foucault highlights the creativity and sense of possibility—social and subjective possibilities, new ways of being—that the proliferation of sexual practices ushers in.

But, I mean, how exciting was it to talk about fist-fucking?! It's not like any of us were into it. It's not like any of us knew anyone who was. Even in the undergraduate demimonde of off-campus housing, few people I knew were having sex with as much regularity as they might have liked, let alone experimenting with the so-called recent proliferation of male homosexual practices. But it was still exciting to talk about it, to outline in theory something that might not otherwise assume a shape either in practice or in fantasy. It was certainly gratifying to imagine that fistfucking had enough conceptual integrity to show up in a theoretical conversation alongside more traditional philosophical concepts like desire or personhood. We debated the desire of things we didn't specifically desire for ourselves. Theory became a site, like porn or sex clubs, to learn about sex, even if that learning confined itself to abstraction.

Even if—but maybe also *especially*. The draw of queer theories like Foucault's or Sedgwick's had something to do with the opportunity for talking about sex and desire—for giving airtime to those things that AIDS and youth conspired to make us feel were so embarrassing—while still keeping the conversation intellectual, hypothetical. Desire became an idea to be debated and discussed, not, or not just, a personal feeling to be displayed in all our hesitancy and inexperience. I talked about sex in academic fora and essays and classrooms, as a theoretical thing, all the time after about age nineteen. But I was well into my thirties before I ever alluded, even elliptically, to my actual, personal sex life in any public or professional context. The former felt enabling, expansive; the latter continued to be tinged by shame long after my own experiences with sex stopped being hypothetical.

From what I can gather, my students today learn about sex from the abundance of internet porn. They will have watched people have sex many times before they attempt any of those same actions themselves.

Porn is their sex education, and if they are curious about fistfucking, without much difficulty they can find videos, Q&As, even tutorials. For my friends and me in our youth, fistfucking was much more an idea, and we loved it as one. But those were the Nineties, when things that were outré became comprehensible without exactly being real, when history drove a wedge between desire and its fulfillment, which theory then helped us to bridge.

* * *

The summer after college, I fell in love. One night, my paramour came over, and we fucked until the early hours of the morning. Then, somehow, holding each other in the sweat-soaked sheets, we got into an argument about the theory of disciplinary power that Foucault outlines in the first volume of *The History of Sexuality*. The argument lasted twice as long as the sex did. I liked this ratio, and this juxtaposition, of the life of the mind and the life of the body. I looked at this boy in the dark and thought, "This could work." For a while, it really did.

4

SEETHING THEORY

In 1966—the same year that Jacques Lacan published his *Écrits* and that Jacques Derrida first met Paul de Man at a conference in Baltimore—Julia Kristeva arrived in Paris as a student from her native Bulgaria. She was on hand to absorb the scenes of theory's postwar French explosion, and three years later, in 1969, Kristeva published her own contribution under the intimidating Greek title *Σημειωτιχή*, with the French subtitle *Recherches pour une sémanalyse*. While the original French edition had the stark white cover that characterized so many Éditions du Seuil volumes, the English version, retitled *Desire in Language* and published by Columbia University Press, which I picked up at a used bookstore about a quarter century later, was black, with gold and white letters framing a cover-dominating black-and-white photo of a young Kristeva. Whereas French readers were invited to contemplate the erudition of the Greek letters, English readers were invited to contemplate the soft lines of the author's face.

Back at the makeshift desk in my college bedroom, I readily complied. It was, I am sure, in some basic sense exciting just to see what a theorist looked like.

Absent image searches, wikis, and similar repositories, I read theory books in the Nineties with only my mental pictures of their authors—and these were often stunningly disconfirmed later when I did come across photos. For this reason alone, the cover of *Desire in Language* made an impression. Beyond that basic fact, though, the Kristeva pictured on the cover looked to young me like an interesting person. With her face resting on her hand, her blouse tugging asymmetrically across her neck, her hair pulled back, but her bangs slightly windswept, the image conjured an intellectual at a picnic or a seaside who nonetheless allowed the leisurely conversation to turn toward some serious contemplation. Her body and gaze angled toward the out-of-frame but also to the near distance, and I imagined her talking to Someone Very Important about matters that I longed to understand. This author photo suggested at once gravity and grace. It was one of the only photographs of an intellectual that I, at twenty, had ever beheld, and tentatively, perhaps without knowing what I was doing or what it could mean, I projected something of myself onto it.

Of course, it's not at all difficult to stand over this book cover and detect a whiff of the kind of sexism by which a woman theorist gets pictured—face, lips, hair, and blouse—while similarly indomitable men like Derrida or Foucault tended not, in the Eighties and Nineties, to likewise grace their own book covers. But sexist as the fact of this cover image might

DESIRE IN LANGUAGE
A Semiotic Approach to Literature and Art

JULIA KRISTEVA
Edited by Leon S. Roudiez

Kristeva, *Desire in Language* (Columbia University Press, 1980)

indeed be, it generated for me, at an impressionable moment in my own intellectual formation, some concrete possibility that a theorist could also be a woman. At stake in the twinning of those terms was something open-ended, something vague though still exciting about the authority behind theory not restricting itself by gender. But I should have begun that sentence, "At stake *for me* . . ." In the privacy of my college bedroom, contemplating book covers and intellectual futures, it was my privilege to value feminism as an idea, without feeling the deep identifications and angers that swirled around it.

Understanding feminist theory provided a singular episode in my education with theory, because it necessitated pitching a tent in an emotional landscape where I didn't have to rest. The value of feminism seemed intuitive to me, and you may not be surprised to learn that I was one of those Nineties guys who declared myself a feminist at every opportunity. At the same time, such declarations didn't cost me much. I valued a set of entirely important political and theoretical ideas that, nonetheless, have a way of staying mostly theoretical when you're living in a body at which nobody is ever going to catcall or whistle as you make your way to class.

And so, despite the fact that I and anyone I knew in college would have regarded our attempts to study feminism as political acts, our education also had an ineluctably sentimental side. Undertaking to master feminist theory set into tension theoretical and political principles, on the one hand, and actual, irreducible felt experience, on the other. We were learning how to feel about gender and power and about their structures, inequities, and pleasures. Moreover, in learning how to feel about gender, we weren't just learning how we as individuals happened to feel; rather, we were learning which kinds of affects the university, and maybe the broader culture, tied to which kinds of political positions. An education in feminist theory proceeded by trying on possible feelings and taking on existing conflicts. These gave us a means to refine our own senses of the ideas and politics we cared about. Accordingly, gender in the Nineties became as emotionally heated an academic topic as there was, and we contemplated it with raised fists and even more raised voices. We yelled. We fought. We seethed.

* * *

There's a lot to be learned from spirited arguments, and the history of theory is full of them. Some are well-known exchanges, like Derrida's disagreement with Foucault's account of madness, followed by Foucault's acid reply that appeared a famously petty nine years later; or Foucault's thunderous silence in response to Jean Baudrillard's call for an outright dismissal of the first volume of *The History of Sexuality*. Other arguments seem to be functions of particular theorists' dispositions, where the common denominator is their personality. Thus, in succession

Freud's collaborators quickly became his rivals, while Alain Badiou picked fights with everyone he met (even notably go-along-to-get-along types like Gilles Deleuze) but after their deaths named them publicly as dear friends; and meanwhile, Lacan made a career out of actions that are more or less the equivalent of the GIF of Mariah Carey saying "I don't know her." But unpleasant as such slights and fights and arguments may sometimes be, they can also be productive. Marx's disputation with Feuerbach produced one of the most elegant and consequential listicles in modern history—including the phrase literally engraved on Marx's tombstone in Highgate Cemetery, London: "Philosophers have hitherto only interpreted the world in various ways; the point is to change it."

There may be a demonstrably productive quality to theoretical arguments, but you also may have noticed that none of the preceding examples, strictly speaking, is about gender. I hasten to add that arguments about gender can of course be highly productive and clarifying for thought. Gender, certainly, is something that has been and can be theorized with great sagacity and sometimes life-changing implications. But gender is not, and never entirely can be, a purely theoretical thing. We have gender and live gender and iterate gender through our actions—we invest in gender for ourselves and others, often in ways in which even very intelligent people can't be fully conscious. We can argue *about* gender, but,

I don't know her

Jacques Lacan's career

by virtue of being people who live with gender in our lives, in our speech, and in our psyches, we are also always to some extent stuck using our gender to argue *about* gender. When that kind of recursive psychic and social terrain becomes the fodder for theoretical argument—when, in other words, we ourselves identify with the things we're arguing about—it's no wonder that people begin to seethe.

Age is a multiplier for these particular theoretical challenges. You can imagine, or you may remember, the acute investments the young feel in their genders. A majority of traditional-age college students are new to adulthood, and little at that age has encouraged them to pry the self-defining questions of how and whether life could make this or that opportunity available, this or that future possible, apart from the coming-of-age experiences that, unless you are uncommonly fortunate, are shaped by gender at every turn.

How to be, how to dress, how to talk, what to talk about, how to act, and whom to fuck: these are all young adult questions—questions, in other words, that young adults are not typically expected to have answered definitively—and all of them are also questions whose answers will be gendered. It makes a ton of sense that such students would be interested to study, discuss, debate, and otherwise theorize gender, but, on the surface, their willingness to do so is different in kind from a willingness to engage with, say, eighteenth-century European painting. As we theorize gender, we inevitably get tangled up in its knotty skeins. At moments we sense ourselves, or some parts of ourselves, to be at risk in the argument, and we argue harder, more forcefully, because the stakes feel higher than usual. It's difficult to be tentative when we feel ourselves to be at stake in an argument, and the seething anger that often erupts in such moments expresses our strident commitment to positions that feel like more than mere intellectual positions. The truth about gender may indeed set you free, but first it will very likely piss you off.

* * *

Kristeva's name circulated in discussions of Eighties feminism, but it was not associated with the biggest arguments of those years, the acerbic debates about women's sex and sexuality that came to be known as the Feminist Sex Wars—that more dubious honor goes instead to Catharine MacKinnon. By the time I was in college in the Nineties, the prosex, proporn, pro-S/M positions in the debate were regularly short-handed as the "anti-MacKinnon" position, though this shorthand, it turns out, was of recent coinage. In fact, MacKinnon was not active in the emerging antipornography foment of the Seventies. She did not become associated with the antipornography movement until around 1983, and her signal and much-cited theoretical essays from the then-leading feminist journal *Signs* in 1982 and 1983 mention pornography only in passing. Instead, MacKinnon emerged from the Seventies with a deservedly brilliant reputation as a feminist legal scholar whose work had consolidated jurisprudence around the newly theorized legal category of sexual harassment. On this basis in 1983 the city of Minneapolis hired her and the feminist writer and activist Andrea Dworkin to draft legislation outlawing pornography on civil rights grounds.

It's worth pausing here to appreciate that as recently as 1983, pornography had not been established as protected speech, and one could still reasonably imagine outlawing or censoring such media in the name of civil rights. A Supreme Court case like *Hustler Magazine v. Falwell* (1988), which upheld the First Amendment rights of pornographers, was still in the future. Pornography was only beginning to become available in the privacy of one's own home, via consumer adaptations of technologies like the VCR and the polaroid, and otherwise its practically Victorian association with vice dens, back alleys, and dark movie theaters still held strong. MacKinnon and Dworkin's understanding of pornography jived with commonsense conceptions and misconceptions about pornography coming out of the Seventies, though they added the argumentative twist that the production and consumption of pornography were discriminatory behaviors that necessarily harmed women.

It's also worth pausing to appreciate that as virulently anti-MacKinnon as was I and everyone I knew in the Nineties, we owed more than we realized to the antiporn feminists. Take Back the Night marches, for example, were (and in many places still are) a staple of feminist organizing and empowerment on college campuses—staging candlelight processions and rallies where women assemble after dark to reclaim space that has historically and culturally been marked as unsafe. But it was only while researching this chapter—that is, basically yesterday—that I learned that the first Take Back the Night march occurred in 1978 in San Francisco, at a rally devoted to antipornography feminism. The zone of overlap in positions like MacKinnon's and the ones we called anti-MacKinnon was not something that the often ferocious arguments between these positions left much room to acknowledge.

The anger that generated the polarizing clarity of positions like pro- or antiporn sacrificed nuance with remarkable efficiency. Accordingly, MacKinnon's antipornography writings from the Eighties are a strange read now, as we all know she's the antiporn enemy of women's sexuality, and yet the astonishing clarity of her critique of structural sexism is nearly unparalleled. One would have to try hard to surpass the eloquent and synthetic account of the nature of gender-based inequality that MacKinnon outlines in the first eight or so pages of her 1987 essay "Francis Biddle's Sister." After those opening pages, however, as the essay pivots to pornography as the cause of all this inequality, the argument strains considerably. MacKinnon is, of course, a legal scholar trying to imagine legal solutions to inequality, and for such an argument, a singular cause is a welcome target. The fact that she set her sights on too singular a cause doesn't exactly mean we should fault her for trying. It does, however, mean that we can (and did!) fault her for getting it wrong. And that, I think, the try-and-fail, is a big part of what made everyone so angry and, consequently, what made the sides of the argument feel so far apart.

MacKinnon became something of a straw woman in debates about women's sex and sexuality, and, oddly, one of the only scholars to take her and Dworkin's antipornography work seriously was a French professor and proto-queer theorist named Leo Bersani. Opening his scandalously titled essay

"Is the Rectum a Grave?" (1987) with the observation, "There is a big secret about sex: most people don't like it," Bersani gave the final third of his argument over to an elaboration of the stakes of antipornography feminism. What he liked about what MacKinnon and Dworkin had to say was their implication that sex itself was a bad thing, that it was already a relation of domination (men over women) that pornography simply eroticized and reinforced as a genre of realism rather than of fantasy. Feminists, Bersani argued, taking MacKinnon and Dworkin's argument to its logical extreme, should reject intercourse and criminalize sex until such time as it can be reinvented.

What Bersani *liked* in other words, was all the arguing, all the friction, and he implied that the sex wars would be well served by even more war and even less sex. "Is the Rectum a Grave?" argues on behalf of a thoroughgoing antipastoral, nonredemptive, account of sex, which has been generative for some subsequent strains of queer theory, and it says something about the politics of Bersani's position in the late Eighties that his essay also includes not one but two backhanded objections to Gayle Rubin's flashpoint essay on the legitimacy of lesbian S/M as a sexual orientation; the very idea of harmless fun between consenting adults is, Bersani implies, itself harmful. The fight is where we learn, he seemed to say, and his essay aligned with some unpopular positions in order to advance the conversation.

In this context, however, the truly odd thing about Bersani's take was its cool commitment to logical argument. It's unmistakable in the essay that things like homophobia and sexism made him angry, but his expression of that anger on the page was, at most, snide, catty, biting. Indeed, one would be hard-pressed to characterize Bersani's essay as one that seethes. Rather, it's a cool and clever take on feminist anger, turning a felt position into more of a logical one. As a young reader who didn't easily get angry, it appealed to me how he values emotions he does not bear. But rereading the essay years later, as a reader who's a little more in touch with my own angers, it's striking, and almost anticlimactic, how much Bersani's writing lacks the emotional tonalities of MacKinnon's and Dworkin's.

* * *

The differences between the Eighties and the Nineties matter a lot for the ways I encountered feminist theory. The book I owned by Kristeva, edited, translated, and published in 1980 as *Desire in Language*, was based on texts published in French between 1969 and 1977. Her more widely read *Powers of Horror: An Essay in Abjection* was from 1980, translated in 1982. Some other of Kristeva's works had been available in English prior, but the Eighties were the moment that they really entered the Anglophone theory catalog. Given the slow movement from a book's publication to its appearance on an undergraduate syllabus, the odds are relatively low of my having been assigned to read Kristeva as a college student had I been ten years older than I happened to be.

It probably also mattered that I was something of a haphazard scholar, reading hungrily for my own purposes and with little regard for chronology. By the time I encountered *Desire in Language*, I had already been reading a lot of queer theory that postdated it. This time-warped (and, frankly, misguided) prelude to reading Kristeva was framed by a youthful reading of other theoretical texts that erred so happily, so misguidedly, on the side of the affirmative: what queer theory opened up, what it made possible. That sense of possibility found amplification in queer theory's open-ended account of how identification and fantasy might catalyze sex and gender (some version of what Sedgwick, as discussed in the previous chapter, designated "gender transitivity," or perhaps what a male college friend once more poetically proposed as "If we were both girls, we'd probably be dating"). Unsystematic reader that I was, I relished the ways that queer theory seemed to validate how my identifications and desires spilled out in multiple directions at once. So I identified—unconsciously but also at moments willfully—with something that Kristeva, as a woman writing theory, seemed to represent: the blouse, the bangs, the big ideas. I imagined this identification was part of the point, and, I guess, it became so.

Was this sort of affirmative queer identification why I wasn't especially angry reading feminist theory? Was it why Bersani wasn't angry? Different kinds of anger, after all, are differently available to different people, and that's true both structurally and personally (hence the cultural tropes of the angry feminist or the angry black woman). It would, at least, not really be possible to sort out which parts of my collegiate attraction to feminist theory had to do with me being a man or being queer or just having the personality I happened to have. Sure, I felt something when I rehearsed some feminist anger as an anti-MacKinnonite, but I also felt something when I admired Bersani's cool take on her and Dworkin's position—even though the anger and its absence pulled in obviously different emotional directions. If my education in feminist theory was allowing me to try on possible feelings and take on existing conflicts, maybe for whatever combination of reasons I also harbored some resistance to those possibilities. Feeling an emotion can be an opportunity, but it can also be a big ask.

It's also possible that at a certain level some of these positions felt like they were important without exactly feeling like they were mine. By the time I was in college, the Feminist Sex Wars were mostly over. Figures like MacKinnon and Dworkin loomed large, but their best-selling books were behind them, and the movement for which they became spokespeople mutated and redirected toward new targets. Surely these circumstances have something to do with the fact that into the late Nineties we studied the Feminist Sex Wars, but we all took the same, prosex, pro-porn, pro-S/M positions. We argued fiercely with enemies whose views had been vanquished. Our argument, seemingly undiminished in its intensity, was nonetheless a leftover argument.

* * *

Feminism in the Eighties argued about gender and sexuality, but before long it was also embroiled in arguments about how to argue. In 1997, Judith Butler published *Excitable Speech*, a culmination of the essays she'd been circulating for several years on the language of injury. One part of the book directly refutes MacKinnon's work, but the parts that attracted the most attention were those that theorized what had become the widespread practice of "resignification." The theory went like this: racism, homophobia, and other forms of discrimination weaponize language and deploy its power against people, and the response to such significations were resignification—moments when people who had been harmed by the power of language took back that language and dismantled its weaponization. So, for example, the people who had been taunted by a homophobic slur like "queer" gradually reclaimed the word and called themselves queer, identified as and with queer, and called their intellectual work "queer theory." They resignified the term.

Ultimately, resignification amounts to a kind of linguistic application for social construction. The latter is a classic social science insight—that behaviors, rituals, and their meanings are culturally specific and vary widely by time and place. From a social constructivist perspective, there is no necessary reason why a word like "queer" is a slur and not a compliment. But there are constructed reasons, and the fact that the word has been a slur is an effect of history and culture, both of which can and do yield, though only very slowly.

The theory is elegant, and it is empowering, but actually doing it often made you sound incredibly angry. In the act of resignifying, one walked around loudly using words that many other people recognized as hateful, offensive, or just inappropriate for polite situations. (Somehow there were many, many more polite situations in the Nineties than there are today.) The fact that by 1997 some people were calling themselves queers did not mean that, say, a politician or a community leader or a university president wanted to be on record using that same word, which some part of their audience might not recognize as a reclaimed term. And though "queer" is now pretty commonplace, in the past five years the Twitter-literate public has seen the same kinds of bottom-up resignifying claims and top-down public hesitations around words like "tranny" and "nasty."

A friend told me a story about his days in a Nineties liberal arts college that captures the point. Someone he knew was giving prospective students—that is, high schoolers and their parents—a campus tour.

As is the convention with such tours, the guide walked the guests through the tree-lined paths and the beautiful grounds, pointing out sights and land-marks, some of which one would never need to enter in four years (the admission office) and some of which someone eager for their life to begin might sheepishly want to know about (the frat house). As the tour group paused in front of a bulletin board advertising a meeting of the queer student organiza-tion, one of the parents took immediate objection. What was the meaning of this? Was such offensive language tolerated here? "No, no," the guide patiently explained to the concerned parent, "'queer' is a word that has been reclaimed." Seeing that the explanation had not registered, she helpfully added, "Like 'cunt.'"

* * *

Though resignification challenges the power behind words, it acts little on the feelings they can carry. Resignifying words like "queer" or "cunt" in real time didn't exactly cancel the force those words held; it just nudged the feelings toward a different register. Add to this circumstance the fact that some of the most spirited theoretical arguments of my youth were left over from the decade prior, and it's not wholly surprising that, in my tutelage by feminist theory, I was a quick study with the theory part but slower, more reluctant, to engage the emotional side.

But then one day, my resistance broke apart all at once. About five years after college, I read a newspaper story one morning about a group composed of graduates and dropouts from UC Santa Cruz, about my age though unknown to me personally, who had founded a kink porn start-up in San Francisco. Asked in the course of the interview about college or other experiences that prepare one for such a career, one person spoke dismissively about feminist theory in particular. In his brief elaboration of the point, however, he conflated the MacKinnonite, antiporn position with Marxist feminism more generally—or, to put it in the terms discussed earlier, he lumped together MacKinnon's pre- and post-1983 work. It made me livid.

By any rational account, I had little reason to be. Here was someone I didn't know, bringing up undergraduate recollections toward which he harbored mere impressions, claiming that those impressions amounted to little more than something he wanted to dismiss. Despite some analytical sloppiness on his part, he nonetheless took an anti-antiporn position, which was approximately mine as well, except that by about 2004 these debates had mostly cooled, and if you'd asked me, I would have told you I didn't really care anymore. These circumstances together would seem to provide wholly insufficient fodder to make me as angry as I nevertheless felt.

Temperamentally disinclined to anger, as I mentioned, I had usually demurred from grounding my feminist politics in that emotional register. But all of a sudden it seemed pretty undeniable that I had access to some feminist rage after all. Perhaps that anger was a delayed reaction from the decade prior. Perhaps what was being dissed had become a thing I used to care about and so, in that sentimental remove, actually seemed mine. It certainly felt like I was holding onto some *something* that this guy in the news story, by contrast, had so glibly let go. But my anger, whatever its cause, does go to show that emotional investments in ideas can run deeper than we expect them to or even feel they should. Arguments may resolve positions, but they also leave remainders.

* * *

Around the same point in graduate school when I was getting angry about a stranger confusing MacKinnon with Marxist feminism, I took a night off to hear Kristeva speak at a bookstore in New York. It was on the occasion of the English translation of the *Colette* volume in her trilogy on "female genius." A friend and I arrived an anxious half hour early, anticipating a crowd that only arrived on academic time, which is to say, in a flood of noisy laughter and bespectacled bodies that poured in on the hour, so that the event might begin five minutes late. My early vantage, however, let me watch the choreography of the event in its planning moments, as the bookstore manager pointed out to the staff who would sit where on the makeshift stage, who would give introductions, who would speak, and in what order.

Kristeva appeared with the rest of the crowd, in a fitted turquoise suit (no asymmetrical blouse here!) and sporting what was unmistakably Chanel Shocking Pink lipstick. Under the bookstore's fluorescent lights, the lipstick brought her features into a kind of severe relief. It perplexed me as it seemed at once perhaps the wrong color on her complexion but equally perhaps well beyond my feeble knowledge of lipstick. It was, in a word, an enigmatic signifier. It located her firmly on a trajectory of feminine beauty and also somehow astride it.

Kristeva's manner that night struck a similar bargain. At first, she demurred to speak in what she claimed to be not-good-enough English, shaking off the event choreography that I had watched the store manager plan. A graduate student pulled from her entourage must, impromptu, speak in her place. Mere minutes later, when the graduate student's description of the female genius project took a turn that was not apparently to Kristeva's liking, she jumped in to correct her and proceeded in accented but in fact flawless English through a measured and perfectly paced account of her recent work. In the course of an hour, Kristeva's language became indistinguishable from her lipstick: each did its signifying work, both as a formal artifice and as a means of communication, signifier and signified working together endlessly forward yet just as endlessly freighted by conventions of culture, of history.

Was she angry at the store manager or the event planners for putting her on the spot? Was she angry at the student for misrepresenting her intellectual project? Would Kristeva have been treated in the same ways had she been a man? Was gender a factor in how she handled uncomfortable circumstances? Or, as Virginia Woolf asked at an entirely different academic event whose social topography nonetheless traced gender's contours, "Who shall measure the heat and violence of the poet's heart when caught and tangled in a woman's body?"

Though these are worthwhile questions, all that they ultimately have in common is that I have no idea how to answer them. I have no idea how I would ever have any idea. I cannot and would never deny that gender was in the room with us, but neither can I precisely point to aspects of the experience that isolated gender or made it visible in some determinate way. Gender is not an efficient cause. The only thing that feels concrete, as I comb my memories of the hour I spent in Kristeva's presence, is the incongruous shade of her lipstick.

It's true that if Kristeva had been a man, I might not have registered or recalled much about her appearance, and this structural sexism that colors my memories annoys me. Whether or not she was angry that night, it turns out that I am, a little bit, at myself. The upshot here is that her lipstick might well be read as a component of a larger intellectual argument. The terms of the argument are not those with which I am most familiar, as it has never, mercifully, been my task in an academic setting to have to negotiate a balance between my professional self and my femininity. But the evening I spent watching Kristeva lecture taught me something about the labor that goes into such a negotiation and also about the impossibility of getting it definitively right.

Kristeva reached an agreement in this negotiation by landing on the side of the feminine, making herself recognizable first as a woman, and tempering that position in the arbitrary symbolic of gender, as needed, with the deliberately secondary fact that she happens to have one of the greatest theoretical minds of any living intellectual. The memory of the event with which I'm left—where I cannot decide whether Kristeva's was among the most brilliant, the most subtle, performances of gender and intellection I have ever witnessed or whether the bookstore's lighting was unforgiving—certainly brings the arbitrariness of gendered signification into high relief.

Who wouldn't be a little angry?

5

STUCK THEORY

If there's one thing that will make any student of theory feel stuck, it's plodding through Jacques Lacan. The brilliant and enigmatic founder of the École Freudienne de Paris was, by all accounts, a god-awful writer. Lacan's talent was instead as an oral teacher. His seminars, promising a "return to Freud" but delivering an often radically new attention to language in psychoanalysis, took place annually in Paris for nearly thirty years, to larger and larger audiences. Only near the end of his seventh decade, according to Elisabeth Roudinesco's clarifying biography of Lacan, did the theorist begin to want things written down. Through his career, of course, Lacan had written, but most of the books that now bear his name are transcriptions, edited and translated, from his oral deliveries. These were his real works.

The main exception is a book of writings called *Écrits*. (In French, *écrits* means "writings." It's not an untranslatable word, but if you leave it in French, you get to sound pretentious.) My college days were those of the old Alan Sheridan translation (the more recent "complete" translation by Bruce Fink was not published until 2006), and the copy I purchased was one that I only very partially read, though I made a lot of jokes about its difficulty (e.g., "You can't read Lacan without Hegel"). After my first semester of graduate school, however, I got it in my head that I needed to understand Lacan better. I sat in coffee shops for a week of my winter break, puzzling through this famously challenging book of essays, making my own index of terms, writing down charts, noting parallels between different concepts, marking the original contexts for some of the famous "out-of-context" phrases I had heard repeated (for example, "desire is the desire to desire").

Reading Lacan that week was uniquely soothing. I remember the feelings of those days vividly, with the comfort and excitement that other people attribute to childhood Christmases. I took pleasure in the ritual of my reading, which was elevated by the feeling of accomplishment when that week and my perusal of the book were both over. I recall the satisfaction with which I folded my page of notes, stuck it into the book, and then (with perhaps more determination than satisfaction) schlepped that book from one apartment to another four times before I had to teach from it years later during my first job after grad school. Only then did I pull out my trusty page of notes and begin rereading the essay I had assigned to my students. It made zero sense. Like, none. I had read it before, knew what it was about, and literally had notes in front of me. Still I was coming up short.

However unintentionally, there is something a little perfect about this story, because to enter into Lacan's terms is always to play with absurdity. He marshaled an arsenal of seemingly paradoxical or self-contradictory concepts, to the glee of his enthusiasts and often to the frustration of his lay readers. To give you just one example, Lacan writes in a number of places about what he calls *méconnaissance*, that is, misrecognition or misconstrual (it's another term his translators usually leave in French). The idea here is that, as a human child is developing its sense of self, what it learns about the world does not always align with the actual reality it sees or senses. Lacan loved to speak of the instance of seeing oneself in the mirror. The child sees the mirror as something out there in the world, but as it grows up, it will learn, like the rest of us, that the reflection in the mirror is itself. For the child to see its mirror image as an external object, instead of reflecting itself back to itself, is a misrecognition, a *méconnaissance*, but—and here's the Lacanian flair for paradox—the misrecognition is also correct. That image is not the child; it *is* outside the self and in the world. Our sense of ourselves relies on making sense of the world in ways that are not identical to our own sensory experiences of it. Or, as Lacan puts it, the self is extrinsic to itself. From this example, I hope it becomes clear that this guy must have been real fun at parties.

(A related example comes from Lacan's actual parties. In 1955, Lacan and his second wife, Sylvia Bataille, purchased at auction Gustav Courbet's 1866 painting *L'origine du monde*. It now hangs in its own room at the Musée d'Orsay in Paris, but if you've never seen it, you may know it by reputation, because it's a realist canvas filled entirely with larger-than-life, disembodied, engorged vulva. The Lacans installed the painting in their country home in Guitrancourt, but not before Lacan commissioned his stepbrother, the surrealist André Masson, to build a double-bottom frame for the painting so that he, Masson, could paint an abstract version of Courbet's painting and position it on top of the original, obscuring the latter from sight. Guests would come to the Lacans' home and see the painting hanging on the wall without actually being able to see the painting itself. Like I said, fun guy.)

Put in my best Lacanian-sounding terms, the question posed by my experience of reading him becomes something like, Was I stuck when I didn't understand what Lacan was saying, or had I been truly stuck in grad school, when I thought I did? With the question posed this way, the Lacanian answer would almost certainly be yes. But the value of that answer—its insight, its provocation—would be based not only on admitting I was stuck either way but on sorting out whether I was better off in one kind of stuckness or another. There's no winning in a Lacanian universe, but there are ways to lose less badly.

* * *

"Stuck" is not a properly psychoanalytic term. I'm not sure it's even a common theoretical term, though it lodged in my vocabulary decisively when I read Lauren Berlant's *Cruel Optimism*. Berlant's book uses the word—as both noun and verb, as well as paronyms like "unstuck"—on a number of occasions and to powerful effect. At the same time, she doesn't gloss it with the sheen of jargon or present it as a central concept. For her, and certainly for the way I have appropriated her term, "stuck" is just a useful means of describing the feeling or the experience of being fixed in place. To be stuck is to be located in happenstance—neither a zone of crisis or trauma nor one of aspiration or desire. By my reckoning, stuckness doesn't generate too much narrative. Ask a stuck person why they live here, and you might be told, "I just do."

Even without being a storied theoretical term, "stuck" is a concept that theory needs. It's not a good thing or a bad thing exactly; it's just a thing, a way of talking about the vicissitudes of ordinary experience. Or to use the least sexy word I have at my disposal for describing theoretical concepts, "stuck," as a term, is mature. It's a word for which one reaches from the middle of something—midargument, midmeal, or (I sometimes fear) maybe just midlife. As such, "stuck" counterposes the more out-of-the-ordinary and phenomenologically singular experiences toward which the vocabulary of theory clusters: terms like "event," "trauma," "aporia," "différend," "exception." Once you begin to take inventory of the way this vocabulary skews away from "stuck," it's tempting to conclude that "stuck" is exactly what theory doesn't want you to feel.

To be sure, the promise of being unstuck was undoubtedly one of the motivations by which theory came into my life, for it corroborated the impulses of youth. For example, one of the many fashions of my college years was veganism. Young people commonly experiment with diet as a way of trying to remake themselves, literally and figuratively. Vegetarianism and veganism were to the Nineties what macrobiotics had been to the Seventies or gluten-free or paleo is to now: all ways to land in both an identity and a practice of self-transformation through food. But veganism wasn't just something we did. As a practice, it begot and, equally, was begotten by theory.

My vegan friends and I argued and agreed about ideology, nonviolence, and the ethics and scales of consumption. In our more far-reaching and self-reflective moments, we thought about the relationship among individual choices, preference, desire, and the big structural mechanisms of things like global capitalism and national agriculture. The theory and practice of veganism were inextricable. We theorized what a just or minimally exploitative consumption might look like and then tried to live it out. As far as we were concerned, every dash of Bragg's Liquid Aminos enlivened debate as much as (honestly, probably much more than) it enlivened a plate of brown rice. We used the vocabulary and the conceptual tools of theory as a way of grafting the entirely ordinary activity of eating onto something much larger and more meaningful. There's a joke that says, if you're trying to figure out if someone is a vegan, don't worry, they'll tell you. Like a lot of jokes, it harbors a note of truth; but only a little defensively would I insist that the act of telling was, in my experience, less about sanctimoniousness than it was the by-product of trying to convince myself, as much as anyone else, of Something Really Important.

Certainly the aspirations of theory, as I have described them here and in the preceding chapters, are transformative. Veganism is just one example of the far-reaching potential of these transformations. The larger point remains that the transformative aliveness of theory is part of why I gave so much of my youth to studying it. From memes and jokes and reading groups to friendship and sex and love to meals and shopping and debate, theory provided an occasion for transformative things to happen. Our actions had *meaning*. Sure, many of those actions might have happened anyway; but they happened in this way, and that quality of the experience makes a difference. By contrast, my life would be impoverished if I had never, say, read *Moby-Dick*, or listened to Nina Simone or come into contact with something else that has become a part of me; but I'm equally sure my life would have gone on. Without theory, however, without the years spent thinking and talking and being and becoming in the ways that theory inspired and captioned, well, I have no idea who I'd be.

This identity-saturating nature of theory has to do with the fact that, while eating and studying and loving and joking are ordinary experiences, having them in proximity to theory meant that my language for talking about ordinary things didn't have to feel merely ordinary. In this way, theory did for me what religion or ideology often does for other people: it enriched the world with words and deeds that added up toward something that seemed like more than something. Theory provoked us to have ideas that reached inexorably toward praxis, the consummation of which we sometimes clearly could and, even more excitingly, sometimes clearly could not see. Theoretical ideas about the lives we were living stretched out on the horizon, and they invited us to follow them in the direction of their vanishing point. Theory animated the possibility that we could be unstuck.

* * *

At nineteen or twenty, my friends and I were not really stuck, not in the ways that life can make you stuck as it goes on (see earlier, re: midlife). Nonetheless, we were acquainted with stuckness, and there was an ambient sense in those Reagan-Bush-Clinton decades that American culture itself had become a little stuck, that we were in a period of retrenchment and backlash against an optimism toward ideas of social perfectibility fondly remembered from just the

other side of the time we'd been born. Theory func-
tioned in our imaginations as a way of making the
Sixties last into the Nineties, a way of circling back to
some purer potential of thought for action.

At the least, it seems like more than a coincidence
that my college friends and I, as well as so many of
the fellow travelers I have met over the years, were
attracted to theory with much the same intensity
that we were attracted to Left politics or punk music
or communal living or vegetarianism or sexual experimentation. It was perhaps the same attraction to
a new world that drew Foucault to sadomasochism;
at least, it made a canny kind of sense that Walter
Benjamin would write lovingly about hashish or that
Gilles Deleuze and Félix Guattari would go to see
Patti Smith play during their one joint trip to Berkeley. Like theory, these expressions and embodiments
were designated as a means of feeling out an original relation to ourselves and each other. Likewise, it
felt familiar and even objectively correct to me when
in 2010 students at Middlesex University occupied
campus buildings in response to their administration's threat to cut the entire philosophy program,
that they did so with protest signs that read, "Yes We
Lacan." These students displayed an impulse shared
by me and my friends in our student days. They were
playing with theory in order to give the idea for a
different world a linguistic shape that, in turn, articu-
lated the actions that might produce that different
world. If there was a raison d'être for theory in the

Nineties, it was that we were going to live out our values. We were going to make the world anew.

To be unstuck meant that theory and practice went together. It's small wonder that one of the language games we played in college was (as I learned years later) called a "snowclone." That term refers to a phrasal template, in which you can substitute a couple of words depending on the context but still generate a recognizable cliché: for example, "x is the new black," where x is anything at all you happen to be talking about. Well, in college, I often found myself saying "x is theory, but y is the practice." Should we study at the coffee shop? Homework is theory, but coffee is the practice. Reading *Gender Trouble*? Antiessentialism is the theory, but performance is the practice. (Yeah, these jokes didn't often land. Repetition and delivery helped, though, as did patient friends.)

This particular snowclone had been in my repertoire for a while before I learned that there was an original phrase at its root. All this time I had been riffing off *Lesbianism and Feminism*, a 1971 pamphlet by Anne Koedt, published by the Chicago Women's Liberation Union, that began with an epigraph attributed to Ti-Grace Atkinson: "Feminism is the theory, lesbianism is the practice." Now, it's been a while since I have had any informed claims on the habits of college lesbians, but that sounds pretty unstuck to me.

* * *

The stuckness of the Reagan-Bush-Clinton decades did come to an end, though not one that seemed possible from the vantage of the Nineties. I graduated college in June 2000 and was barely two months into graduate school when the Supreme Court handed victory in the presidential election to George W. Bush (who, we said with a sincere contempt, toward which I feel unendingly rueful, was no worse than his opponent, Al Gore). Ten months later, two airplanes flew into the World Trade Center towers in New York, 185 miles from where I was sitting, at that same moment cramming a chapter from Jürgen Habermas's *The Inclusion of the Other* for the first meeting of a theory seminar I was taking in the Political Science Department. It was not Habermas, however, who came to mind when my boyfriend called from work and told me to turn on the television. I watched the second tower fall and thought about Gilles Deleuze. "So this," I said, "is a becoming." I don't remember whether I spoke aloud.

Deleuze had spent the Sixties writing deliberately provocative interpretations of canonical figures in European philosophy: David Hume, Baruch Spinoza, Henri Bergson, Friedrich Nietzsche. His slim 1963 book on Kant treats all three of the monumental *Critiques* in a spare one hundred pages—a formal polemic if ever there was one. Around 1970, Deleuze began cowriting with the activist-psychoanalyst Félix Guattari, who had spent the preceding decade as an auditor in Lacan's seminars and as a patient on his couch; working together, Deleuze and Guattari's joint ideas became impressively unhinged. Their lengthy and lapidary 1980 book *A Thousand Plateaus*, while not new during my first semester of graduate school, had become all the rage. The previous winter, possibly the same happy week I spent reading Lacan in coffee shops, I paid a visit to a beloved independent scholarly bookstore in downtown Santa Cruz, and I noticed that the proprietor had stocked nearly all Deleuze's books—a change from even six months before. "Are people reading these all of a sudden?" I asked. "All of a sudden," he repeated.

Transformations happen all the time, but the question is how. Deleuze and Guattari explain the process of "becoming" as a particular kind of transformation, which they eagerly distinguish from imitation or analogy. On their account, becoming is, rather, generative of truly new ways of being that are a function of influences rather than resemblances. Key, here, is that the world as it already exists can be reassembled into something that's genuinely otherwise. 9/11 was arguably a "becoming," in Deleuze and Guattari's sense, because it was an occasion when something that was possible but hadn't really happened before (not in this place, not in this way) did happen, and the world reassembled itself in the wake of that event. A becoming makes things unstuck, and the events of 9/11 made aspects of the world literally molten.

In the significantly more minor register of my own life, the events of that morning fomented a different becoming, as I mumbled about Deleuze, maybe out loud, to an empty room. I had spent my college years using the language of theory to make the stuckness of life feel more mobile, but now I reached for a theoretical term to stabilize something. I called it a "becoming" because I needed the event to feel discrete, comprehensible. That need would only amplify in the weeks and years that followed, when the ordinary became otherwise than it had been and so many of my habits of comprehension atrophied, while other latent senses very slowly, lamely began to find expression in words.

Here was the event, unstuck from the vicissitudes of the ordinary. My theoretical vocabulary wasn't good enough to make sense of it. My language failed.

* * *

Nothing about Lacan's writings could solve this problem, but it's also no wonder I was drawn to them. The theorists who ranked among the pillars of psychoanalysis—Lacan but also Sigmund Freud, Jean Laplanche, and Melanie Klein—wrote things that I read with only tepid curiosity in college. But suddenly in graduate school, psychoanalytic theory became interesting in wholly different ways than it ever had been before. I needed its language, which, among other things, offered up the possibility that language was sometimes all we had and also, at many of the same times, was not enough.

It makes all kinds of intuitive sense that I would be drawn to psychoanalytic theory in such times, but I am also hard-pressed to explain where I got the idea to be. Even among theory heads, psychoanalysis was not entirely fashionable coming out of the Nineties, at least not in the United States. Around the literary humanities, the critical language of that moment was infused with the concept of "culture," drawn from anthropology, from the Birmingham School of cultural studies, and from the diffusion of Marxism, via the Frankfurt School and via Foucault, into studies of the "context" for literature—what we learned to call "literary production." Psychoanalysis was not off the table, but by comparison to these other, more prominent strains of theoretical inquiry, it looked like a bourgeois retreat from the historical realities of the post-1989 collapse of actually existing socialism. Yes, those were really the words we used.

While canonical psychoanalytic theory was largely out, one strain in particular, trauma theory, dominated in the Nineties. Properly psychoanalytically speaking, a "trauma" is a psychic disturbance, something that doesn't kill you but that comes close enough that it's not easy to recover from. The word in ancient Greek means "wound," though it is the same in English as it was in Freud's German. He used the word early and often, and some of his readers have argued that its meaning inflected differently over the course of his career. But "trauma theory" changed the word's meaning again. Its rubric named a conversation that tried to emphasize, and to some extent isolate, trauma as a dimension of psychoanalytic theory—that is, to treat trauma not in relation to other pieces of the Freudian ecology of mind (like the death drive or the Oedipus complex) but as a broad analytic in its own right.

The impulse to talk more about trauma in these years did not belong to theory alone. Indeed, few technical theoretical terms have ever leaked into the American cultural imagination as thoroughly as "trauma." In the Nineties, the word was everywhere, and it meant nearly anything. Being in a car crash was a trauma, but so was the AIDS crisis, so was child neglect, so was the Holocaust, and so, according to several Kantian-inflected inquires, was the sublime. Never mind that the actions that catalyzed these experiences—let alone the experiences themselves—were so incommensurably different. Trauma in those days was often measured without a scale, leaving the weight of one kind of experience to balance with any other, whether it was highly personal or broadly sociological.

All these meanings for trauma amounted to a minor trauma in their way, and some scholars tried to salve this terminological mess. Shortly before I took a graduate seminar with the historian Ruth Leys, she published *Trauma: A Genealogy*, whose careful and clarifying history of the term's many meanings dissolved, in the final chapter, into an extreme reaction to Cathy Caruth's then-very-recent book *Unclaimed Experience.* Leys is not exactly wrong to find that Caruth has what nearly any version of psychology would consider an overly literal account of trauma (that trauma, according to Caruth's deconstructive argument, stands outside representation), but neither is she exactly nice about it. "Trauma" was a term that had lost its critical and diagnostic precision well before 1996, and despite my professor's intervention, that fact would only become more and more true as the Nineties ended and a cloud of toxic dust erupted and slowly settled over lower Manhattan.

* * *

People insist now that the justification for the 2003 US invasion of Iraq made sense at the time; but I was there, and I remember perfectly that it didn't. People just trusted, or wanted to be able to trust, the chimera of order that the US government symbolized. Nobody really wanted to abandon the possibility that things made sense, and, accordingly, it made so much sense that an action would have a reaction that people willingly looked past the fact that invasion was pretty obviously the wrong reaction. The siege began on the twentieth of March 2003, just about seventeen months after 9/11. We were all still traumatized. That isn't a precise explanation, but neither is it an incorrect one.

* * *

Amid this mishegas, when the impulse to read psychoanalytic theory came over me, I turned to the small shelf of books by contemporary practitioners, often coming out of the European academy, whose versions of psychoanalysis and psychoanalytically inflected social theories were interesting to American academics: the likes of Jacqueline Rose, Adam Phillips, Joan Copjec, and Slavoj Žižek. What was refreshing about these scholars is that they had read widely in philosophy and theory, but they kept psychoanalysis front and center while avoiding both the devoutness of Freudianism and the messiness of trauma theory.

Reading in this vein of psychoanalytic theory was rewarding, but it didn't make me unstuck, because it did not offer what I really needed—something that, in 2001, was not yet on offer. Only about five years later would that needful thing come into its own as what has come to be called "affect theory." It's difficult to explain affect theory in any summary way, because it's less a theory proper and more like an ongoing interdisciplinary conversation. One of its most useful insights—the one my plaintively outstretched hand could not close around in the fall of 2001—is that emotions are not solely the province of people, but, rather, they belong to larger structural and historical patterns. Sure, people have emotions, but from the vantage of much of affect theory, it's equally the case that emotions have people. Feelings are individual and private, but individuality and privacy are historically contingent social constructions; and so it follows that the things you happen to be feeling are yours but not yours alone. Or, as the academic-activist group Feel Tank Chicago put the matter much more succinctly in that Prozac-saturated first term of the second Bush administration, "Depressed? It might be political."

One of the major conversation openers for affect theory was Eve Kosofsky Sedgwick's 1997 essay "Paranoid Reading and Reparative Reading; or, You're So Paranoid You Probably Think This Introduction Is about You." In the sophisticated but still playful way that the title indicates, Sedgwick's essay explored the fact that, around 1997, insight in the humanities often amounted, à la Adorno, to exposing some hidden machination, some secret working of ideology, and bringing it to light. Against this mode, which she termed "paranoid reading," Sedgwick proposed the alternative of "reparative reading," the possibility that scholars might take pleasure in the objects of our study, that we might be drawn to study because it's a way of giving attention to something that nourishes us, and it is in turn something whose flourishing we may want to encourage. Here as in much of her published writing, Sedgwick wanted to use criticism to promote thoughtful attachments to a wider-than-was-common array of objects of study.

The uptake of these insights was significant both in its reach and, unfortunately, in its delay. Only after the 2003 republication of this essay in Sedgwick's monograph *Touching Feeling* did "reparative reading" become a term of art that critics (at least within my hearing) readily discussed. Sedgwick's intervention was already necessary in 1997, but, like so many things one needs, having it didn't mean that anyone knew what to do with it.

The ballooning interest in affect theory in the past decade suggests that I was not alone in needing it during the decade prior. But absent its conceptual models, I spent the debilitating dark age that people shorthand as "post-9/11" depressed without having any language to explain convincingly that it might be political. Psychoanalytic theory was my best shot, but all it really gave me was some validation for not having the right words.

Of course, validation matters, even if it too is not unsticking. Browsing for the right words I lacked, one day in the school library, I found an edited collection called *Languages of the Unsayable*. I brought it home and kept it for years without ever reading any of the essays. The book meant a lot to me, but the knowledge it imparted was confined wholly to the totem of its title. How comforting it was to imagine that there might be a whole language for the things that one could not find the words to say.

* * *

Not having the right words to describe a new world made me feel stuck, but so, in turn, did other people's insistence that we could continue to use the same old words. For about five years after 9/11, I would read prefaces to newly published academic books that informed me that recent unanticipated geopolitical events made the subject of the book at hand "more urgent than ever." It didn't matter what the subject of the book actually was. I understood such topical indifference to mean that this claim was not literal so much as it was a reflex, a rhetorical tic. At its heart was a desire to carry on with the analysis unaltered or the language unchanged.

The theoretical language we had left over from the pre-9/11 world was not sufficient to a number of aspects of the post-9/11 world, as the variously mute and gaping or else clichéd and empty—in short, the entirely human—responses to the event of 9/11 had themselves proven. But recourse to that left-over language provided a feeling of continuity, and it was continuity that we actually wanted, even if our still-cherished theoretical vocabularies prioritized other kinds of expression. "More urgent than ever" parroted the rhetorical idiom of an event-and-exception-filled theoretical language, but as a tic, it more modestly, more desperately expressed a set of feelings that hovered somewhere between being stuck and not wanting to be.

The scenario in which one does not have the right language is well anticipated by many theories besides psychoanalysis, one of which I had confronted in college. It numbered among my favorite nuggets of theoretical insight gleaned in those undergraduate years, and it came from the opening to Karl Marx's *Eighteenth Brumaire of Louis Napoleon*. Marx is explaining the political coup of 1851–1852, in which Louis Napoleon seized legitimate republican power in order to establish the French Second Empire, much as his namesake and uncle, Napoleon Bonaparte, had done previously in 1804. This text originates Marx's oft-quoted line about how history happens first as tragedy, then as farce. But the passage that caught my attention was a more enigmatic one: "The social revolution of the nineteenth century cannot take its poetry from the past but only from the future. It cannot begin with itself before it has stripped away all superstition about the past. The former revolutions required recollections of past world history in order to smother their own content. The revolution of the nineteenth century must let the dead bury their dead in order to arrive at its own content. There the phrase went beyond the content— here the content goes beyond the phrase." The content goes beyond the phrase. It's not exactly clear what Marx means here—interpreters have debated it—but I was compelled by the idea that an event in the present might exceed the language of the past. Revolutionary things would happen first, and we'd decide how to talk about them second.

The events of 9/11 or the misbegotten invasion of Iraq were, of course, not revolutions. Nonetheless, they were events for which my theoretical language proved inadequate. Marx's "poetry of the future" had anticipated this possibility—as had Deleuze and Guattari's "becoming," as had Lacan's *méconnaisance*—but in all these cases, the content going beyond the phrase turned out to be much, much easier to imagine as a thought than it was to endure as a feeling. For me, at least, reading all those "more urgent than evers" engendered feelings that were blistering, ugly, and awash in bile. I grew truly to hate the ways others seemed to retreat from the hard work of making new language adequate to the overwhelmedness of the event. Now, I'm not certain at whom I was really angry, insofar as my frustration was with everyone else's inability to do something that, at the same time, I also could not do.

Looking back to Marx as a way of trying to look to the future, maybe I was just engaged in a different grandiose futility. All I can tell you for sure is that as I dialed into my 56k modem to access the online library catalog or whatever other website where I might gather my resources for making all those new phrases whose contents I was sure we needed to get beyond, I did so via an AOL dial-up service for which my screen name was "poetryofthefuture." In fact, all my screen names and internet handles in those days were some derivative of this phrase, whose contents I had clearly, manifestly, and, though I couldn't see it at the time, rather literally not gone beyond. It was my own tic. I was holding fast to a vain hope for the ongoing relevance of my theories, just as were the people I was criticizing. In retrospect, I really doubt it mattered that mine happened to be slightly different theories.

* * *

Whatever else my interest in Lacan turned out to be, it was not especially world building. Over the years, I've discovered that when one reads or teaches Lacan, it's remarkably challenging to get people on board if they aren't already among the converted. His prose is so difficult that reading groups often turn out to be more work than fun. In addition to the challenges of Lacan's writing is the strangely exclusive idiolect of the ideas—all the terms that translators leave in French (or worse: German). By contrast, you can read Marx, find it valuable, and maybe even land some zingers about exploitation—and still not be a Marxist. (A college friend swore she was just a little Marxish.) But somehow if you take the trouble necessary to really read Lacan, you end up being a ride-or-die Lacanian. All the more foolhardy it would seem that I was reading Lacan for what was more or less the opposite reason, in the hopes of getting unstuck.

To some extent, Lacan seems to have cultivated the exclusive atmosphere that surrounded him. In 1953, he broke with the Parisian psychoanalytic establishment where he had spent nearly his whole career, over what came to be called the "variable-length session" or "short session." Whereas Freud had established the length of an analytic session as the famous fifty-minute hour, Lacan proposed that analytic insight could be concentrated if the length of a session were shortened at the discretion of the analyst—sometimes to mere minutes. Such unorthodox timing scandalized the Société Parisienne de Psychanalyse, and Lacan and many of his colleagues left to found a different organization.

It's worth appreciating that an abrogation in the contract between the analyst and analysand laid the foundation for Lacan's new analytic organization. In a way, this break was Lacan's becoming—it was, at least, the event that transformed him into the leader of what was suddenly legible as a movement. Lacan's seminars had begun in 1951, but only surrounding the events of this break, in 1953, did they begin to be recorded and, subsequently, transcribed and published (under the sole authority Lacan vested in his protégé, Jacques-Alain Miller, who, in 1966, the same year as the publication of *Écrits*, married Lacan's daughter, now the philosopher Judith Miller). Lacan, meanwhile, both assumed and, from the position of his assumption, resisted this role as leader. He described his seminars as a "return to Freud," and almost three decades later, at a conference in Caracas, he announced that his auditors might be Lacanians if they wished, but he was a Freudian.

It would seem that Lacan's life's work was to fold the already deckled edges of rupture and continuity onto each other until they held together well enough that one had to face the texture of their relation.

Even among theorists, he had the power to make awkward terms and absurd ideas stick. This power did not, however, insulate him from the mechanisms of paradox that he so skillfully wielded, and so, even as Lacan masterfully related things to one another, other things broke apart. Thoughts and feelings can be encouraged to work together, but they are not finally coextensive. Love, Lacan was fond of repeating throughout his 1957–1958 seminar, is giving something you don't have to someone who doesn't want it. I can think that this definition is astonishingly correct and still feel, or want to feel, otherwise. For what it's worth, I have often considered what it might be like to anticipate fifty minutes of someone's time and attention and then, without warning, get only seven. It might be the kind of twist or provocation that yields great insight, but I don't suppose that the abruptness of the technique feels particularly good for the patient. The knowledge that comes with disappointment is great, but it is also partial.

The example of Lacan illustrates—as would the example of Marx or Deleuze and Guattari or many theorists besides—that theoretical language gives us ways to comprehend the world in even its most extreme and unexpected manifestations. But as we use this language to inch our way toward the better world where theory and practice coordinate in an original way, we run into innumerable instances when this language is not enough. In these instances, we often find ourselves stuck with something that doesn't work in the ways that we might need it to, or, perhaps, we find ourselves stuck in a moment when our need might be greater than the means we have at our disposal to satisfy it. For all its rhetorical designs on the likes of "events" and "exceptions," for all its gravitational pull toward the new and the ideal, theory ultimately offers no positions that are immune from these possibilities. Any position is a place where you can get stuck.

Does reading Lacan leave us stuck, or were we stuck already? The Lacanian answer would be yes.

CODA

The five feelings that govern the preceding chapters showcase some of the various ways that theories never exist apart from histories and contexts, events and debates—just as theorists never think, and students never read, entirely apart from their own experiences and desires, actions and foibles. Affect theorists may concentrate on thinking things about feeling, but all of us inescapably feel things about thinking—despite, or perhaps due to, the vast range of things that could count as either thinking or feeling.

But, as I said in the beginning, contexts have a way of shifting. There's no doubt that the university is a major context for student learning, and at present much more than in the Nineties, the university's precipitating crises—ballooning tuition, adjunctification of faculty, assaults on academic freedom, and national student-loan debt topping $1.5 trillion as of 2018—too are coming to bear on the study of theory. I'm not saying, of course, that anyone needs political crisis to dignify their theoretical investigations. Instead, it's been the argument of the preceding chapters that the value of engaging with theory can be exploratory, open-ended, experimental. And it's in that spirit that—now that certain kinds of political crisis are unmistakably here—there might be value in regarding some of the ways that theory creatively weaves through, against, and beyond this context.

In 2009, when the University of California, the largest public university in the world, announced that it would undergo massive budget cuts and no longer serve its mission of admitting the top ten percent of graduating high school seniors in the state, students responded with a manifesto. Called "Communiqué from an Absent Future" and published online, it offered a withering assessment of the social, political, and economic value of university education in the present time. Echoing Marx's rhetoric and Foucault's analyses of power, the manifesto invited people to think and dream and demand alternatives.

This use of theory as an engine for student demand is not new. In 1969, for example, a radical collective at UC San Diego, whose members included Herbert Marcuse and Angela Davis, issued demands for a new residential college that would employ both theory and practice to transform education. The collective lobbied to name the college in honor of the Congolese Independence leader Patrice Lumumba and the Zapatista revolutionary Emiliano Zapata and to organize its curriculum around the theory of political revolutions, economic systems, and the study of whiteness. Though their bid was ultimately unsuccessful, its focus on the legacy of whiteness and colonialism on college campuses, in the names of buildings, and in the curriculum proved remarkably forward-thinking.

Elsewhere in the world, political actions that followed from events like those of May '68 looked not only forward but also backward, to the activities of the Resistance during the German occupation. Resistance tactics were taken up by the abolitionist Groupe d'Information sur les Prisons (GIP), which staged a number of demonstrations outside and even inside prisons in the early Seventies and whose participants included multiple generations of intellectuals like Michel Foucault, Gilles Deleuze, Daniel Defert, Hélène Cixous, Jacques Donzelot, Jean Genet, and Jean-Paul Sartre. Historical resistance and avant-garde thought stood and fought a common enemy, in the name of a better world.

These brief examples suggest that political feelings do theoretical work whether they're extemporaneous or citational or both at once. It was as inheritors of such varied uses for political feelings that I understood the students at the University of Missouri, at Yale, at Ithaca College, and then all over the country in the fall of 2015 who began to sound loud objections to what was euphemistically called the "racial climate" of their universities. These students protested against the naming of buildings around their institutions after racist and sometimes slaveholding individuals (including John C. Calhoun at Yale and Woodrow Wilson at Princeton). They demanded that universities not simply treat diversity as an admissions game but instead grant vital educational, psychological, and financial support to all students who come to learn, no matter where from. Students also made bold demands that curricula be decolonized, so that whiteness not be the default identity of the authors and thinkers taught in universities. They wanted the complicated economic ties that many older universities have to slavery and the native lands on which campuses were built to be acknowledged, assessed, identified, and reckoned with. These students didn't claim to know the endgame of these discussions, but, hearteningly, not knowing did not and does not stop them from making demands for a different world. They are trying to follow a theory and see where it goes. Like the rest of us, they are feeling their way.

Acknowledgments

Thanks to Sarah Blackwood and Sarah Mesle for founding *Avidly*, for making space, for asking me to write this, and for teaching me how.

Thanks to the folks who cluster around *Avidly* for all the warmth and brilliance and feeling they lend to the practice of criticism, especially though far from exhaustively, Mandy Berry, Lisa Beskin, Hester Blum, Tim Cassedy, Michelle Chihara, Lara Cohen, Brian Connolly, Pete Coviello, Ashon Crawley, Greg Edwards, Ramzi Fawaz, Jonathan Flatley, Stephanie Foote, Beth Freeman, D. Gilson, John Havard, Glenn Hendler, Briallen Hopper, Yahdon Israel, Claire Jarvis, Evan Kindley, Grace Lavery, Dana Luciano, Tina Lupton, Sarah Miller, Justine Murison, Jordy Rosenberg, Dana Seitler, Caleb Smith, Gus Stadler, Kathryn Stockton, Pam Thurschwell, Kyla Tompkins, Cindy Wu, and Catherine Zimmer.

Thanks to the team at NYU Press, especially Andrew Katz, Martin Coleman, Dolma Ombadykow, and Eric Zinner.

Thanks to Alexander Lee Testere for the frontispiece illustration.

Thanks to the very patient people who taught me to read theory: Blaize Wilkinson, the late Greta

Slobin, Daniel Selden, Ann Lane, the late Peter Euben, Sam Frost, Robert Reid-Pharr, Bill Connolly, Jane Bennett. One hundred and eight bows to Jody Greene, for all that and handstands too.

Thanks to Rei Terada for finishing a sentence, not to mention all the things she helped begin; to Lauren Berlant for the queer worlds she enables and sustains; to Sianne Ngai for the gifts of her intelligence, humor, and interest.

Thanks to Noah Glassman, in whose conversations thoughts and feelings take shape as stories.

Thanks to Hilary Emmett for going to see Kristeva with me years ago. Thanks to Peter Coviello, Sam Draxler, Ian Epstein, Geoff Gilbert, Andrea Lawlor, Eng-Beng Lim, Dana Luciano, Heather Lukes, Molly McGarry, Meredith McGill, Jasbir Puar, Tim Stewart-Winter, and Ed Whitley for swapping tales and otherwise opening up the archives of their theoretical educations to me. Different versions of some of these stories have been told elsewhere: in *Avidly* and in the zine *FAQNP: A Queer Nerd Publication*. My gratitude especially to Ray Cha for giving me the chance to recollect.

Thanks to the friends who listened to these stories, shared their own, and read: Rahne Alexander, Shonni Enelow, Abby Kluchin, Janet Neary, Julie Orlemanski, Frank Pasquale, and Ben Wurgaft.

Thanks to my students who, over fifteen years and counting, have taught me so much. Especially big shout-outs to Spencer Everett and Adam Fales for sharing the scenes of their learning with me, for reading these pages, and for teaching me the most.

Thanks to Elan Abrell and Delci Winders for making Santa Cruz first possible and then home.

Thanks to the cast and crew of the Cosmic Condo, Robert Chang, Courtney Miller-Callahan, Michael Stevens, and also Rahne Alexander, Heather Malcolm, Janet Neary, Kellie Schmitt, Gloria Shin, and Jesse Silva.

Thanks to Aufie for countless writing breaks and for more than words can say. Thanks to Robin Riley and Newton for walks in the park and rides in the stroller.

Thanks to Edward Hui, for everything.

Works Consulted

Books and Essays

Adorno, Theodor W. *Minima Moralia: Reflections on a Damaged Life.* 1951. Trans. E. F. N. Jephcott. London: Verso, 1974.

———. "The Stars Down to Earth: The *Los Angeles Times* Astrology Column." *The Stars Down to Earth and Other Essays on the Irrational in Culture.* Ed. Stephen Crook. New York: Routledge, 1994. 46–171.

Adorno, Theodor W., and Max Horkheimer. "The Culture Industry: Enlightenment as Mass Deception." *Dialectic of Enlightenment.* 1947. Trans. John Cumming. New York: Continuum, 2001. 120–167.

Anderson, Benedict. *Imagined Communities: Reflections on the Origin and Spread of Nationalism.* 1983. Rev. ed. New York: Verso, 1991.

Anzaldúa, Gloria E. *Borderlands / La Frontera: The New Mestiza.* San Francisco: Aunt Lute, 1987.

Barthes, Roland. *A Lover's Discourse: Fragments.* 1977. Trans. Richard Howard. New York: Farrar, Straus and Giroux, 1978.

Benjamin, Walter. "Goethe's Elective Affinities." *Selected Writings, Volume 1: 1913–1926.* Ed. Marcus Bullock and Michael W. Jennings. Cambridge, MA: Harvard University Press, 1996. 297–360.

Berlant, Lauren. *Cruel Optimism.* Durham, NC: Duke University Press, 2011.

————. *The Queen of America Goes to Washington City: Essays on Sex and Citizenship*. Durham, NC: Duke University Press, 1997.

Bersani, Leo. "Is the Rectum a Grave?" *October* 43 (Winter 1987): 197–222.

Buck-Morss, Susan. *Dreamworld and Catastrophe: The Passing of Mass Utopia in East and West*. Cambridge, MA: MIT Press, 2000.

Budick, Sanford, and Wolfgang Iser, eds. *Languages of the Unsayable: The Play of Negativity in Literature and Literary Theory*. Stanford, CA: Stanford University Press, 1987.

Butler, Judith. *Bodies That Matter: On the Discursive Limits of "Sex."* New York: Routledge, 1993.

————. *Excitable Speech: A Politics of the Performative*. New York: Routledge, 1997.

————. *Gender Trouble: Feminism and the Subversion of Identity*. New York: Routledge, 1990.

————. "Imitation and Gender Insubordination." *Inside/Out: Lesbian Theories, Gay Theories*. Ed. Diana Fuss. New York: Routledge, 1991. 13–31.

Butler, Judith, Ernesto Laclau, and Slavoj Žižek. *Contingency, Hegemony, Universality: Contemporary Dialogues on the Left*. London: Verso, 2000.

Caruth, Cathy. *Unclaimed Experience: Trauma, Narrative, and History*. Baltimore: Johns Hopkins University Press, 1996.

"Communiqué from an Absent Future." *We Want Everything* (blog), September 24, 2009. https://wewanteverything.wordpress.com/.

Crimp, Douglas. "How to Have Promiscuity in an Epidemic." *October* 43 (Winter 1987): 237–271.

Davis, Angela Y. *Angela Davis: An Autobiography*. New York: International Publishers, 1974.

Deleuze, Gilles. *Kant's Critical Philosophy: The Doctrine of the Faculties*. 1963. Trans. Hugh Tomlinson and Barbara

Habberjam. Minneapolis: University of Minnesota Press, 1984.

———. *The Logic of Sense*. 1969. Ed. Constantin V. Boundas. Trans. Mark Lester with Charles Stivale. New York: Columbia University Press, 1993.

Deleuze, Gilles, and Félix Guattari. *A Thousand Plateaus: Capitalism and Schizophrenia*. 1980. Trans. Brian Massumi. Minneapolis: University of Minnesota Press, 1987.

de Man, Paul. "Autobiography as De-facement." 1979. *The Rhetoric of Romanticism*. New York: Columbia University Press, 1984. 67–81.

Derrida, Jacques. *Limited Inc.* Evanston, IL: Northwestern University Press, 1988.

———. "White Mythology: Metaphor in the Text of Philosophy." *Margins of Philosophy*. 1972. Trans. Alan Bass. Chicago: University of Chicago Press, 1982. 207–271.

Dosse, Francois. *Gilles Deleuze and Felix Guattari: Intersecting Lives.* 2007. Trans. Deborah Glassman. New York: Columbia University Press, 2010.

Dreyfus, Hubert, and Paul Rabinow. *Michel Foucault: Beyond Structuralism and Hermeneutics*. Chicago: University of Chicago Press, 1982.

Eribon, Didier. *Michel Foucault.* 1989. Trans. Betsy Wing. Cambridge, MA: Harvard University Press, 1991.

Fanon, Frantz. *Black Skin, White Masks*. 1952. Trans. Charles L. Markmann. New York: Grove, 1968.

Foucault, Michel. "Friendship as a Way of Life." 1981. *Ethics: Subjectivity and Truth*. Ed. Paul Rabinow. Trans. Robert Hurley and others. New York: New Press, 1997. 135–140.

———. *The History of Sexuality, Volume 1: An Introduction.* 1976. Trans. Robert Hurley. New York: Vintage, 1978.

———. "Sex, Power, and the Politics of Identity." 1982. *Ethics: Subjectivity and Truth*. Ed. Paul Rabinow. Trans. Robert Hurley and others. New York: New Press, 1997. 163–173.

————. *The Use of Pleasure: Volume 2 of the History of Sexuality.* 1984. Trans. Robert Hurley. New York: Random House, 1985.

————. "What Is an Author?" *Language, Counter-Memory, Practice: Selected Essays and Interviews.* Ed. Donald F. Bouchard. Ithaca, NY: Cornell University Press, 1977. 113–138.

Habermas, Jürgen. *The Inclusion of the Other.* Ed. Ciaran P. Cronin and Pablo De Greiff. Cambridge, MA: MIT Press, 1998.

Halperin, David M. *Saint Foucault: Toward a Gay Hagiography.* New York: Oxford University Press, 1995.

Henderson, Danielle. *Feminist Ryan Gosling: Feminist Theory (as Imagined) from Your Favorite Sensitive Movie Dude.* Philadelphia: Running, 2012.

Kant, Immanuel. *Anthropology from a Pragmatic Point of View.* 1798. Trans. Victor Lyle Dowdell. Carbondale: Southern Illinois University Press, 1996.

————. *Critique of Practical Reason.* 1788. Trans. and ed. Mary Gregor. Cambridge: Cambridge University Press, 1997.

————. *Critique of Pure Reason.* 1781/1787. Trans. and ed. Paul Guyer and Alan W. Wood. Cambridge: Cambridge University Press, 1998.

————. *The Metaphysics of Morals.* 1797. Trans. and ed. by Mary Gregor. Cambridge: Cambridge University Press, 1996.

Kierkegaard, Søren. *Fear and Trembling.* 1845. Trans. and ed. Howard V. Hong and Edna H. Hong. Princeton, NJ: Princeton University Press, 1983.

Koedt, Anne. *Lesbianism and Feminism.* Chicago: Chicago Women's Liberation Union, 1971.

Kristeva, Julia. *Colette.* 2002. Trans. Jane Marie Todd. New York: Columbia University Press, 2004.

————. *Desire in Language.* Ed. Leon S. Roudiez. Trans. Thomas Gora, Alice Jardine, and Leon S. Roudiez. New York: Columbia University Press, 1980.

———. *Powers of Horror: An Essay in Abjection.* 1980. Trans. Leon S. Roudiez. New York: Columbia University Press, 1982.

Lacan, Jacques. *Écrits: A Selection.* 1966. Trans. Alan Sheridan. New York: Norton, 1977.

———. *Écrits: The First Complete Edition in English.* 1966. Trans. Bruce Fink. New York: Norton, 2006.

———. *Formations of the Unconscious: The Seminar of Jacques Lacan, Book V.* 1998. Trans. Russell Grigg. Cambridge, UK: Polity, 2017.

———. "Séminarie de Caracas." *L'Ane* 1 (July 1981).

[Lawlor, Andrea]. *Judy!* 1.1 (Spring 1993). http://www.qzap.org.

Lemon, Lee T., and Marlon J. Reis, eds. *Russian Formalist Criticism: Four Essays.* Lincoln: University of Nebraska Press, 1965.

Leys, Ruth. *Trauma: A Genealogy.* Chicago: University of Chicago Press, 2000.

Lorde, Audre. "Uses of the Erotic: The Erotic as Power." *Sister Outsider: Essays and Speeches.* Trumansburg, NY: Crossing, 1984. 53–59.

Macey, David. *The Lives of Michel Foucault: A Biography.* New York: Pantheon, 1993.

MacKinnon, Catharine A. "Feminism, Marxism, Method, and the State: An Agenda for Theory." *Signs* 7.3 (Spring 1982): 515–544.

———. "Feminism, Marxism, Method, and the State: Toward Feminist Jurisprudence." *Signs* 8.4 (Summer 1983): 635–658.

———. "Francis Biddle's Sister: Pornography, Civil Rights, and Speech." *Feminism Unmodified: Discourses on Life and Law.* Cambridge, MA: Harvard University Press, 1987. 163–197.

Marx, Karl. *The Eighteenth Brumaire of Louis Bonaparte.* 1852. *The Marx-Engels Reader.* 2nd ed. Ed. Robert Tucker. New York: Norton, 1978. 594–617.

———. "Theses on Feuerbach." 1888. *The Marx-Engels Reader*. 2nd ed. Ed. Robert Tucker. New York: Norton, 1978. 143–145.

Miller, James. *The Passion of Michel Foucault*. New York: Simon and Schuster, 1993.

Müller-Doohm, Stefan. *Adorno: A Biography*. 2003. Trans. Rodney Livingstone. Malden, MA: Polity, 2005.

Ngai, Sianne. *Our Aesthetic Categories: Zany, Cute, Interesting*. Cambridge, MA: Harvard University Press, 2012.

Peretti, Jonah. "Capitalism and Schizophrenia: Contemporary Visual Culture and the Acceleration of Identity Formation/ Dissolution." *Negations*, Winter 1996. https://www.datawranglers.com/negations/issues/96w/96w_peretti.html.

Ronell, Avital. *Stupidity*. Urbana: University of Illinois Press, 2002.

Roudinesco, Elisabeth. *Jacques Lacan*. 1994. Trans. Barbara Bray. New York: Columbia University Press, 1997.

Rubin, Gayle. "Thinking Sex: Notes for a Radical Theory of the Politics of Sexuality." *Pleasure and Danger: Exploring Female Sexuality*. Ed. Carole S. Vance. New York: Routledge and Kegan Paul, 1984. 267–319.

Sedgwick, Eve Kosofsky. *Epistemology of the Closet*. Berkeley: University of California Press, 1990.

———. "Paranoid Reading and Reparative Reading; or, You're So Paranoid You Probably Think This Introduction Is about You." *Novel Gazing: Queer Readings in Fiction*. Ed. Eve Kosofsky Sedgwick. Durham, NC: Duke University Press, 1997. 1–37.

———. *Touching Feeling: Affect, Pedagogy, Performativity*. Durham, NC: Duke University Press, 2003.

Spivak, Gayatri Chakravorty. *In Other Worlds: Essays in Cultural Politics*. New York: Routledge, 1987.

Stoler, Ann Laura. *Race and the Education of Desire: Foucault's History of Sexuality and the Colonial Order of Things*. Durham, NC: Duke University Press, 1995.

Wade, Simeon. *Chez Foucault*. 1978. https://progressivegeographies.files.wordpress.com.

———. *Foucault in California*. Berkeley: Heyday Books, 2019.

Watney, Simon. *Policing Desire: Pornography, AIDS, and the Media*. Minneapolis: University of Minnesota Press, 1987.

Wittig, Monique. *The Straight Mind and Other Essays*. Boston: Beacon, 1992.

Woolf, Virginia. *A Room of One's Own*. 1929. San Diego: Harcourt Brace, 1981.

Films

Derrida. Dir. Kirby Dick and Amy Ziering Kofman. Jane Doe Films, 2002.

Happiness. Dir. Todd Solondz. Good Machine, Killer Films, 1998.

Hedwig and the Angry Inch. Dir. John Cameron Mitchell. Killer Films, New Line Cinema, 2001.

Tongues Untied. Dir. Marlon Riggs. Signifyin' Works, 1989.

Watermelon Woman, The. Dir. Cheryl Dunye. Dancing Girl, 1996.

About the Author

Jordan Alexander Stein teaches in the English Department and the Comparative Literature Program at Fordham University. He is the coeditor (with Lara Langer Cohen) of *Early African American Print Culture* (2012), and his critical nonfiction has appeared in *Avidly*, the *Awl*, the *Los Angeles Review of Books*, *Salon*, and *Slate*.